Secrets of Highert Contact, Release Your Cosmic Power and Flying Saucer Revelations: The New Age Trilogy

Michael X Barton
Kenneth Arnold

SAUCERIAN PUBLISHER

ISBN: 9781736731444

© 2021, Saucerian Publisher

Al rights reserved. No part of this publication maybe reproduced, translate, store in a retrieval system, or transmitted in any form or by any means, electronic, mechanical, photocopying, recording or otherwise, without prior written permision from the publisher.

FOREWORD

It is generally a good idea to return to the classics in any genre. This also goes for UFO literature. Rereading a book, or reviewing old documents after ten or twenty years is a rewarding experience. You will discover new data and ideas you didn't notice before. The reason, of course, is that you are, in many ways, not the same person reading the book the second or third time. Hopefully you have advanced in knowledge, experience, intellectual and spiritual discernment. A good starting point is to reread the contactee classics material of the 1950s, in order to understand the deeper mystery involved in what happened during that era.

Contactee is the name that has been given to people, especially since the 1950s, who claim contact with extraterrestrials, beings from other planets. In the wake of the citing of flying saucers by pilot Kenneth Arnold in 1947, speculation was rampant that they were possibly spaceships from a distant planet . This group included George Adamski (1891–1965), the pioneer, and his quickly emerging competitors: Truman Bethurum (1898–1969), George Van Tassel (1910–1978), Daniel W. Fry (1908–1992), Orfeo Angelucci (1912–1993), George King (1919–1997), Buck Nelson (1894–1982), and about as many others, more obscure. The era came to an abrupt end in the US with Betty Hill (1920–2004), who introduced a new paradigm to replace Adamski's stereotypical Space Brothers.

Following the Adamski tradition, one of the most influential contactees of that era was a man named Michael Barton, who wrote several books under the pen name of Michael X. Michael Dimond Barton was born on May 26, 1937 in Seattle, Washington, and died on June 26, 2003 in Los Angeles, California. He was the son of Claude Coffee Barton, and Elva Lois Dimond. He had a brother: Jerry Keith Barton. He died on June26, 2003 in Los Angeles, California. There is not much information about Michael X Barton available. Here is a brief biographical note taken from the edition of *Secrets of Higher Contact:* Michael X. Barton is widely know for his New-Age writings, and has been a prolific author in the Metaphysical and Inspirational field since 1949. Thousands of persons from all walks of life,who are seeking higher Truth and Wisdom, find a wealth of New-Age Information and guidance in his easy-to-read writings.In 1940, Michael's own inner development was accelerated in a dramatic and, positive way, when he was contacted briefly by a white-garbed Master from the higher planes of life. Michael's inner eye was opened temporarily and he could see the Being clearly. From this time on, Michael pursue the Higher Truth. He organized and taught a "Self-Unfoldment" class in 1960, with great success. In 1961, Michael X, Barton received the honorary degree of Doctor of Divinity from Dr. John W. Hopkins, president of Williams College in Berkeley, California, Michael is also a fully ordained minister of the Universal Life Church of Modesto, California. "Michael" is alse known for his interesting and informative lectures on New-Age topics, He has spoken to attentive audiences in many cities in California, Arizona and Nevada since 1954. A fascinating column, entitled, "A Look in The Crystal", which appears as a regular feature in the *Cosmic Star* newspaper, is written by Michael. In 1964, a "Cosmic Visitor" apparently from a much higher dimension than our own limited three-dimensional world, cortacted Michael. The contact was made by a vision, in full color, in which the "Visitor" revealed his presence to Michel. This Cosmic Being gives no name, but states tha: he is "the Truth, the Light, and the ALL in the Universe." The Visitor is entirely REAL. He is responsible for an amazing phenomenon (a picture of an Angel in an old print called The First Christmas Morn, has been weeping real tears frequent intervals since 1961), and other supernormal manifestations. The Cosmic Visitor has made a tremendous PREDICTION. It concerns an impending COSMIC event that will be world-transforming! Michael X. Barton's thrilling book entitled, "The Weeping Angel Prediction", tells the full story of the Cosmic Visitor and his prophecy, and documents many of the incredible manifestations now occurring all over the world. Michael X Barton is not a spokesman for any earthly Church system of religion, "My ministry," he says, "is Universal Trulh and Higher Evolution".

Saucerian Publisher was founded with the mission of promoting books in Science Fiction, Paranormal and the Unknow. Our vision is to preserve the legacy of literary history by reprint editions of books and magazines which have already been exhausted or are difficult to obtain. Our goal is to help readers, educators and researchers by bringing back original publications that are difficult to find at reasonable price, while preserving the legacy of universal knowledge. This title is an authentic reproduction of the original printed text in shades of gray. **IMPORTANT.** Despite the fact that we have attempted to accurately maintain the integrity of the material, the present reproduction may have minor errors beyond our control like: blurred paragraph, poor pictures from the original scanned copy.

Because this book is culturally important, we have made available as part of our commitment to protect, preserve and promote knowledge in the world. This book is an authentic reproduction of the Barton's following titles:

Secrets of Highert Contact
Release Your Cosmic Power
Flying Saucer Revelations

Great, but unpretentious, these titles are an extraordinarily rare symbols by themselves of what was going on in those early years of the modern UFO era.

Editor
Saucerian Publisher, 2021

TABLE OF CONTENTS

Secrets of Highert Contact	2
AUTHOR'S FOREWORD	3
Part One *Saucer Mystery Unveiled*	4
Part Two *Brothers of The Higher Arc*	10
Part Three *Contacting Your Secret X*	16
Part Four *How To Uplift Others Now*	20
Part Five *Will You Be a Contactee?*	23
Part Six *Your Most Important Role*	26
Part Seven *Space Brothers Need YOU Now!*	28
"THE COSMIC QUESTION BOX"	32

RELEASE YOUR COSMIC POWER — 35

FOREWORD — 36

Part 1
"Chaos Ahead For The Masses!" — 37

Part 2
"How Is Your Cosmic Balance?" — 42

Part 3
"The Cosmic Balance Secret" — 45

Part 5
"Each One Reach One" -- NOW — 53

Part 6
"Your Cosmic Power Program" — 55

STORING UP SOLAR — 56

THE BEST "SOLAR" FOOD — 57

HOW TO SET UP YOUR PROGRAM — 58

Part 1
"Releasing The Cosmic Power" — 60

IN-DRAWING THE COSMIC ENERGY - (Practice No. 1) — 61

PROJECTING THE ENERGY TO OTHERS (Practice No. 2) — 62

RELEASING THE COSMIC BALANCE LIGHT 63
(Practice No. 3)

DIAMOND STAR MEDITATION 63
(Practice No. 4)

Flying Saucer Revelations 67'

The Saucer People on Earth 68
Mystic Monograph No.1

SAUCER PEOPLE ON EARTH 69
Part One
Man's Secret Origin

THEN THE EARTH SHOOK TERRIBLY! 73

THE AIR FORCE NOW BUILDS ITS OWN 74
FLYING SAUCERS

A PERSONAL NOTE 75

SAUCER PEOPLE ON EARTH 76
Part Two
The Contacts

Flying Saucers at Giant Rock 81
Mystic Monograph No.2

FLYING SAUCERS AT GIANT ROCK 82
Part One
Out of This World

FLYING SAUCERS AT GIANT ROCK
Part Two
Wisdom of the Cosmos — 87

Secrets of the Saucer
Mystic Monograph No.3 — 93

SECRETS OF THE SAUCER PEOPLE
Part One
The Venusians — 94

SECRETS OF THE SAUCER PEOPLE
Part Two
Secrets of the Universes — 99

The Magic of Ether Ships
Mystic Monograph No.4 — 104

THE MAGIC OF THER SHIPS
Part One
The Etheric World — 105

THE MAGIC OF THEIR SHIPS
Part Two
The Great Harvest — 110

Disk, Destiny & You
Mystic Monograph No.5 — 116

A PERSONAL NOTE — 117

DISK, DESTINY & YOU
Part One
The Polar Shift — 118

A VISION OF THE IMPENDING — 121

SPECIAL NOTE — 121

DISK, DESTINY & YOU
Part Two
Your Secret Destiny — 122

Secrets of Higher Contact

by
Michael X

"SECRETS OF HIGHER CONTACT"

- by -

MICHAEL X

* * *

This is an Educational and Inspirational Course of Study... especially written and intended for NEW AGE Individuals everywhere. The following SEVEN Chapters are contained herein:

1. "THE SAUCER MYSTERY UNVEILED"

2. "BROTHERS OF THE HIGHER ARC"

3. "CONTACTING YOUR SECRET X"

4. "HOW TO UPLIFT OTHERS NOW"

5. "WILL YOU BE A CONTACTEE?"

6. "YOUR MOST IMPORTANT ROLE"

7. "SPACE BROTHERS NEED YOU NOW!"

* * * * * * *

Statements in this Course are based on Scientific and Super-Sensory Findings. No claim is made as to what the information cited may do in any given case and the Publishers assume no obligation for opinions expressed or implied herein by the author.

AUTHOR'S FOREWORD

"SECRETS OF HIGHER CONTACT" was written at the definite request of our Space Brothers. It is intended especially for you -- the New Age individual -- to uplift and guide you on THE PATH OF THE HIGHER CONTACT.

The complete technique by which you may reach up into the high consciousness of the Interplanetary Beings and contact them, is revealed for the first time in this book. The Brothers -- "Beings of the Higher Arc" -- considered it unwise to reveal certain details of the "Higher Contact" before we were ready.

"SECRETS OF HIGHER CONTACT" contains some of the best information I have been privileged to give in my lectures. It also brings you the latest, up-to-the-minute ideas, conclusions and instructions for your important NEW AGE activity in the service of others.

A new phase of the Great Plan is now under way. Activity on the Flying Saucer horizon has not ended. It is just beginning! Our Higher Brothers now wish to make conscious contact -- via Telethot (special Thought Transmission) with many thousands more of us New Age Individuals on Planet Earth.

Your important part in this wonderful New Age activity is outlined herein. You are about to open a Door into a fabulous universe. Proceed carefully and cautiously, following instructions closely. Do not try to rush things. Allow yourself time to unfold this new and wonderful experience.

                                              MICHAEL X
                                              Seer of The New Age

SECRETS OF HIGHER CONTACT

Part One
The Saucer Mystery Unveiled

A special Message given by Michael X to a wonderful group of New Age Individuals at Park Manor Hotel in Los Angeles, California, Oct. 9, 1959

* * *

BLESS YOU, EVERYONE! It's so inspiring to be here and to see you again, and to feel the warmth of this group tonight. It certainly thrills my soul. And in this feeling, this uplift that I have been joyously receiving from you, I am confident that what will come forth tonight will be something we shall all remember for a long time.

I pray that the Master that guides me shall be with me tonight. And I ask that he place his hand upon my shoulder-- give me Light and Strength to share with you. We know -- you and I -- that he will be here.

Since 1947 when Kenneth Arnold made the first important sighting of Flying Saucers in the United States, a vast number of sightings and "contacts" have been reported by many persons. You and I realize that a great many of these reports have been based -- not on fact -- but on overwrought imaginations and inaccurate observation. People have thought they were viewing flying Saucers when in reality what they were viewing was high altitude jet planes, balloons and in some instances the guided missiles of our Armed Forces.

Also, a certain amount of fraud has reared its ugly head in the Flying Saucer picture. Some of the stories of contacts with the Space People have been hoaxes. Sometimes the motive behind the hoax has been mercenary, and sometimes the motive has been to gain a sense of "self-importance" in the eyes of the world. All of us know of such cases.

But in spite of fraud, money-grubbing, and distortion of the truth, a large number of these reports of sightings and contacts have been made by reliable, intelligent and honest people. Capable people whom we love and respect, such as engineers, scientists and important individuals in every walk of life. These individuals KNOW the TRUTH. They know that this planet we live on is being visited by interplanetary craft manned by intelligent beings from other worlds!

And in spite of it all...In spite of so many "imagined" sightings and contacts and fraudulent stories that we have heard to date, all of these things are being used by the ALL Father to further His purpose in these times. The sightings have served the special purpose of AWAKENING the good people on earth to the BIG CHANGES that are coming. Yes, He has been preparing His own, His Elect people for the Dawn of the Day now imminent. The Great Day of this our planet earth.

Now tonight, we are going to talk about the Secrets of Higher Contact. Many of you sincere New Age Individuals have been asking, "How can I contact the Space People?" You want to know HOW to actually become a "Contactee" so that you too will communicate -- as a select few others on our planet are now doing -- with higher intelligences from other worlds.

I assure you IT CAN BE DONE. If your motive is right, you can make higher contact. But, and this is the only real "catch" to it...If your motive is wrong, that is, if it is primarily selfish, you will only make lower contact. That is where so many otherwise sensible persons get sidetracked. They forget to put their little "small-self" will aside, so that the Higher Self in them can act in its pure, noble and unselfish way.

Your High Self is not in the least interested in small or petty aims. It is not interested in personal "self-importance" either. What really matters most to it is whether you are perfectly sincere and honest in your wish to serve the universal forces of Life, Love and Light. Sincerity and honesty enable us to unfold and progress faster on THE PATH.

Many well-meaning persons are "in contact" with lower intelligences and, sad to say, are not even aware of the situation. You may perhaps know of someone who believes he (or she) is in communication with some advanced being from another planet, but the truth might be just the opposite. Some mischievous and wily entity--a lower type of intelligence on the astral plane of our own planet earth--may be posing as a Martian, a Venusian, Jupiterian, Saturnian, etc.

Let me make myself entirely clear on this point. Not all spirits are good spirits. They are not all necessarily good, wise and honest. There is a great astral realm surrounding the earth, and this realm has its lower regions and its higher regions. The lower astral regions are inhabited by beings of less spiritual development than the beings who dwell in the higher levels of the astral realm. Some of these low astral beings like to "masquerade" as wise and superior intelligences and they say to many would-be contactees that they are the higher space people. And many people are being deceived. The deceived ones then go about unknowingly deceiving others.

The reason why these lower intelligences get away with their trickery is easy to understand. They are always on the lookout for foolish men and women with BIG EGOS. Anyone who is puffed up with "small-self" importance is fair prey for those clever astral entities who play on the individual's vanity, pride and basic selfishness. They wedge their way into one's consciousness through the ingress of a bloated ego. Then the lower entities USE that individual to further their own unsavory purposes.

How can you protect yourself against those dark forces? By your MOTIVE. Let it be in line always with the upbuilding forces that exist within all creation. That is easy enough to do, once you become imbued with the spirit of HIGH ADVENTURE! Yes, that's the key to it. HIGH rather than low. To seek the HIGH self -- the Oversoul as Emerson described it -- is our objective. Reach for Soul-Contact first. Then, it will be utterly impossible for you to go wrong or contact the wrong type of space intelligences. Your vibration will be too high for them.

That spirit of high adventure in your soul is constantly lifting you upward if you will respond to it. It's always bringing you just the right experiences that will help you develop the beautiful SOUL within you. So reach with me for the "High Consciousness", and with this attitude, with this approach, we shall demonstrate the ideals of High Thought, High Word and High Deed in all that we do.

Then, we find ourselves moving onward, upward and Godward instead of merely marking time. Our higher vibrations will be just right for making contact with the genuine Space Masters, our spiritually advanced Brothers and Sisters of the more highly evolved worlds. We won't allow ourselves to get sidetracked and delayed on the astral plane. We want to "by-pass" that lower level and reach up to the high contact. From then on, our joy will be boundless.

Service to the Great Plan of the ALL-Father, which the Brothers themselves know and serve, is the crying need of our planet and its people today. The need is -- TO SERVE. And we can all serve the Father's Great Plan best by making a determined effort to reach up for Soul-Contact first. Then, by consciously cooperating with the Hierarchy of Wise Ones in every way that is shown us in our day-to-day lives.

Whatever the Brothers call you to do in these times, by all means put your best foot forward. This is what you and I have waited all our lives for, to lose ourselves -- our little selves, that is -- in a HIGH and NOBLE CAUSE! The time is NOW, and the cause is that of UNIVERSAL UNDERSTANDING!

We have the great opportunity now to cooperate with the Higher Beings in bringing about the Great Plan. That Plan is unfolding according to schedule. We know that the appearance of the flying saucers in our skies in the past few years has been an important part of the Plan. Since 1947 there has been a vast number of true and valid sightings. They have now served their purpose. They have brought about a certain spiritual AWAKENING in the souls of New Age Individuals all over this planet.

Of course, the "mass-minded" have missed the main point of it all. They are still looking for sensation and physical phenomena. But the Brothers are not trying to convince the masses of anything, nor are they concerned with converting any of the skeptics. there isn't time for that. They are, however, greatly interested in reaching the "awakened ones", individuals like yourself because you are teachable.

At the first annual Convention of AFSCA (Amalgamated Flying Saucer Clubs of America) which Gabriel Green held at the Statler-Hilton Hotel here in Los Angeles, the Brothers let us know they and their ships are not "imaginary".

On the very day of the Convention, Flying Saucers were sighted over Hawaii! Perfectly timed for the Convention... remember that? Newspapers carried front page headlines!

So these Higher Beings exist! They are real, advanced human beings, exalted beings with a tremendous intelligence. They know how to time events precisely. And they know how to carry out a great over-all plan for greater human good.

The very fact that you are here tonight; the very fact that I am here tonight is part of a higher plan. A truly spiritual plan that we have the opportunity and privilege to voluntarily cooperate with. No one is imposing their will upon us. Least of all the Higher Brothers. They never impel nor impose their will at any time. Each of us has free choice as individuals. We may choose or reject.

If we can see the Plan more clearly, then of our own free choice we can lay the "small-self" will aside, on the Altar of the ALL-Father. Then the higher will and purpose of the Father begins to work through us. And this is truly the highest wisdom, because the small-self possesses very little wisdom, actually. Far, far grander wisdom exists beyond it!

The Space Brothers say that what we call our "human will" is really only an illusion. The automatic working of the natural law of action and reaction (karma) knocks out the concept of human will. Only the Universal Will exists.

You and I know that every action always brings a reaction, and the reaction is good or not so good depending on the nature of the act. No matter how we try, we cannot avoid the consequences of our actions...but happily we do have a free choice. We can carefully choose our actions.

And when we choose to act according to Higher Self direction, rather than from Lower Self "mis-direction", the higher Will of the Father works through us. With its magnificent power, wisdom, light and love and joy, we are then lifted higher and higher on the TRUE PATH. We UNFOLD THE GOD IN US. It's thrilling, isn't it? And wonderful!

Why then, are the Space Brothers here? Why have the Flying Saucers been seen? The answer now appears that it was to awaken the planet. It was to awaken us (who are now ready to be awakened to our higher destiny) to the fact that we are now in the Last Days of the Old Era. The Piscean Era is fast coming to its closing, and now the New Era -- the Golden Age of Aquarius -- is about to unfold in all of its grandeur and glory.

They -- our Space Brothers -- are here to help us because we are sick. WE ARE SICK WITH KARMA! NEGATIVE KARMA! Karma being the strong reactions from destructive actions we have committed in the past on this planet Earth! There has to be a healing, loving, enlightening force brought in to our world to neutralize the negativity and bring a state of balanced equilibrium NOW.

From that new state of balance, where Light, and Love and Joy predominate, we can function in a healthier condition. We can then become attuned to the Universal Will. In this way we shall find our place in this particular time.

And each of you HAS a particular place -- a unique and special function -- because you are a New Age Individual! You have a high responsibility in these times to serve only your highest ideals. To become a Soul-Center of Light and Love and Joy more radiant and powerful than ever before, so that you can be of greater assistance in the days ahead. I know the Brothers need you and me...and we need them!!

THE TIME OF SIFTING HAS NOW ARRIVED

This is now a great Sifting Time on planet Earth. The Lambs are being steadily sifted from the Goats. Edgar Cayce as he spoke through my beloved friend Betty Nuss, mentioned this -- that the Sifting Time is here now. All of the spiritually awakened souls (the Lambs) on earth are being separated from the goats who are blissfully asleep to the reality of their spiritual nature and the Great Plan.

Those who have become awakened souls -- the Lambs -- will be enabled to assist the Great Army of Light in the unfolding of the Great Plan for humanity. You and I as New Age Individuals will become mighty forces for bringing about that Higher Plan.

A great Cosmic Cycle of time is drawing to a close, and our planet is getting ready for something higher, better and far nobler than anything it has ever known. The big changes coming will mean a step upward for this earth and its people. It will all be brought about in as gentle and natural a way as possible...for that is the way the Higher Forces work.

These are conclusive days that we live in now. When the realization of this fact reaches your inner self, are you fearful? Don't be. You must let go of fear and replace it with joyous love and gratitude for all that is in the Plan. Conclusive days, yes. But not the days to walk with fear. For you and I have a greater opportunity in these times than we have ever had in all of our previous lives on earth! An opportunity to walk in the light, love and joyous awareness that we are -- all of us -- "watched by angels", and that they are working with us and for us as we REACH UPWARD.

THIS IS THE TESTING TIME "Many shall be purified," made white and tried at this time, as never before. Tried to see IF they can be relied upon as responsible co-workers in the "vineyard of the ALL-Father". Now to be a reliable co-worker means simply this: That we voluntarily offer to lay our personal "small-self" will upon the Altar of the Sacred Spirit -- the Divine Spark within us. We set the little human self aside, and ask the Higher Self to take control. That is what it means.

Giving up the little self-will is not easy to do. Few of us can release it all at once. Each day we have to give up a little more of "human mask" of personal "self-importance" and desires of the personality, for something BIGGER, BETTER, AND ETERNAL. We are not ready for HIGHER FREEDOM until we place our Divine Spirit in control for only it is FREE.

In our new freedom we go into ACTION...here and now. We apply what is given to us, each step of the way. Deeds, not words are most important to your progress and mine. We go into action at once to purify ourselves, to cleanse our etheric bodies, to lighten and transmute our bodies of flesh. Remember, we are gradually entering into a New Dimension on this planet Earth. It will become a planet of higher vibratory frequency, of more etherialized matter. We cannot rush things. But we can and should move with the Cosmic Tides... and with courage prepare now to move into new dimensions.

SECRETS OF HIGHER CONTACT
Part Two

Brothers of The Higher Arc

Soul-Contact is the MOST IMPORTANT thing we could possibly do at this time for ourselves and for others. This is so vitally important now. Why? Because the High Self intelligence of each individual is his or her best teacher and guide.

Your soul is able to communicate with the High Self, and carry on a two-way conversation with it. Thus will you receive the most valuable higher wisdom and guidance. For it is the still, small voice speaking within you that can lead, guide and direct you clearly in the way you should go as you travel THE PATH.

With such divine guidance -- for it is actually the voice of God speaking to you -- darkness and confusion is dispelled and you move swiftly on the true path of LIGHT.

At this time -- as the Old Piscean Age is rapidly drawing to a dramatic ending -- walking with those in the Light is important. Walking in the Path of Light is very important. And walking in the Path of Love...that is MOST important! Love is the Key to reaching up into the High Consciousness. Yes, it is a fact. Higher Contact is made only by those who love, for love lifts us into a very high awareness.

Many New Age Individuals are sending a great vibration of pure love out to other human beings at this time. This is most helpful, for as we realize, the "Sifting" of human souls is now going on. During this Sifting Period we try to help the "goats" to come up into a higher state of awareness.

Only a very few of them will understand and respond. As for the others of the "mass-minded" men and women, they will not understand what is going on right under their very eyes. But you -- and all other New Age Souls -- you shall understand. You shall keep faith with your teachers and with your higher self. The human goats will continue moving in circles because they are depending on physical, material senses only. They must see, hear, touch, smell and taste in order to believe.

Unhappily, such persons are "trapped" in matter. They lack <u>inner</u> vision to see the spiritual realities that exist behind material things. When "D-Day" - Diploma Day -- comes, those spiritual laggards will not be entitled to a "Diploma" attesting to sincere, higher service to mankind; because no such service has been rendered by them. But do not feel undue concern over those souls. No soul is ever lost in the Great Plan. Laggard souls are simply "harvested" by the Etheric Beings in charge of such things, and taken to a planet in another solar system where conditions are more in keeping with their "slowpoke" nature. On that less evolved planet the backward souls will "take the work over".

You, the New Age Individual, by your study and practice of these higher teachings, are spiraling up beyond the "trap" of dense matter and its limitations. You are moving upward into a faster vibration to where the Light from your High Self can pour through you in ever-increasing radiance!

Soul-Contact then, is the next step to take. And the magic of higher contact is simply this: That first of all, before seeking to contact the Saucer Beings, we are to make genuine contact with our own Soul. Via the Soul, we reach upward to make contact with the High Self intelligence.

Then, having done that -- and we do it by daily practice of certain techniques of Light now being revealed to all the faithful -- the other contacts with Saucer Beings will follow in a natural, easy sequence of steps.

Each of you has a most wonderful opportunity now to become a more perfect and useful "channel" for the Light, and a marvelous "receiver" of higher communications. According to your sincerity of motive and desire to be of service to the "Brothers of the Higher Arc" will you become a center -- a living center of Life, Love and Wisdom.

In this regard I must speak of the Subliminal State of mind. It has an important relationship to higher contact. The Subliminal state is a condition of "conscious plus Subconscious awareness". When you acquire the art of relaxing your physical body completely, you find that your mind gains greater freedom. Although your conscious mind is still to some degree active, your deeper mind, the subconscious, is most active. Gradually it begins to function throughout the entire brain. You are no longer hampered by little hindering ideas, and soon you experience a HEIGHTENED AWARENESS.

Edgar Cayce, the Seer of Virginia Beach, became quite proficient at entering into the "Subliminal State" of mind. That state led him gently into the higher, or "Superconscious State" of mind. "Super" meaning above and beyond, or a higher state of awareness. Wisdom then poured through him and he was enabled to assist many thousands of sincere individuals, by giving them psychic readings as to the real nature of their physical ills, and the best means of treatment.

In my earlier book entitled "Venusian Secret Science", the complete technique of getting into the subliminal state was presented in easy-to-understand step by step procedure. Those who haven't yet learned this important technique which is very basic to any contact with the higher forces, should secure this valuable information as soon as possible.

Now, we come to a very interesting subject: Definitions. How do we define "Space People"? For some time now, many of us have used the term "Space People" or "Space Beings" in referring to all beings who travel in the Flying Saucers and in the various types of spacecraft. This is true; these are "Space people" defined as those who are able to travel safely in outer space. The fact is, however, that there are many different kinds of beings who inhabit space. Human beings, for example, who have attained mastership over matter by working knowingly with Light (and that includes mastery of their finer bodies) are able to lay aside the heavy material body and travel in a mental body. They can then move with the speed of thought. All space is their home and they do not require physical or etheric spacecraft in order to navigate anywhere in our solar system. Can we not call these "Space People" also?

There are also Etheric Beings. These are human dwellers on the various etheric planes in the universe. They live in worlds just as real to them as ours is to us, but they have no dense material flesh body as we do. These, too, are space people.

There are also the WATCHERS. In the Holy Bible they are called "Watchers from a far country". They are physical human beings very similar to us, whose home is not on earth but on some other material planet in our solar system. In order to reach our planet they use spacecraft of an advanced type which are capable of interplanetary flights. Although they have physical bodies, they are of a much higher vibratory frequency than most earth bodies and are far more "etherialized".

Most of these Watchers come from the more highly evolved planets such as Venus, Mercury and others. They have been observing our planet since 1947 in a most intent manner. As you have already learned, they are aware of the critical condition our planet is in now that it has the secret of atomic power. Atomic radiation due to the many atom bomb tests has caused more havoc than most of us realize. But that is not all.

We now live in a COSMIC TIME. Our entire solar system is entering a new and higher region of light. Changes of a cosmic nature are definitely due for this planet and for us.

In the days of Noah people were told to "flee to the high mountains". Now we are not told to flee to the mountains but rather to "stand in the Holy Place". Where is the Holy Place? It is within you. It is the Sacred Shrine that each individual now must build within himself. For within that Shrine shall come the "telepathic call", the warning, the guiding and the leading from your own High Self Intelligence.

Divine direction will come. Your responsibility and mine, is to diligently train ourselves to be better "receiving sets" for higher thoughts and impressions. In ancient times the word given Ezekiel was: "Behold, Son of Man, I set thee a Watchman to warn my people!" Yes, the Watchman will warn us at the proper time. But it will be an inner warning, an inner voice rather than an outer voice. And it will come through the mechanism of your own awakened Soul.

We said that these are conclusive days. Magnificently big changes are impending. The Brothers of the "Higher Arc" are far more aware of the nature of these changes than we are. That is why many high and noble beings from extremely high and spiritual realms are coming to our planet, and why they have been observing our world for so long. They desire to be near this earth, to better assist us in these conclusive days. And here is a most important point.

These High Brothers I now refer to are Etheric Beings. But they come from an Etheric level infinitely higher and more refined in Etheric Density than any of those surrounding this planet earth. Their order of intelligence is far greater, and far more spiritual than anything known to us.

These wonderful Beings have made the great sacrifice of taking on themselves an Etheric body much denser, and much heavier than the fine spiritual bodies they normally wear. They themselves do not call this a sacrifice...but they say that perhaps you or I would term it that. They use denser bodies to be near us at this time. It is not easy nor comfortable for them to be in earth's lower vibrations, but as it is necessary for us to be guided, they have come.

They are near us, guiding us, leading us. Why? To enable all sincere souls to perfect themselves and enlighten others. As we do this, we shall realize what St.Paul was speaking of when he said: "And we which are alive (in our higher frequency perfected bodies) will be caught up into the air to meet Him." This event is the "Great Airlift" spoken of in the Bible and in other sacred books.

If each one here tonight will put forth the sustained effort that is required to REACH THE HIGH CONSCIOUSNESS, I assure you that you SHALL make the grade! Your spiritual light will begin to shine with ever-increasing brightness. THAT bright light will positively attract the attention of the "Brothers of the Higher Arc". They'll see your light and draw closer to you. Then high contact will become a reality to you. A glorious, living reality. YOU WILL THEN BE A "CONTACTEE". And all your doubts will be gone.

The Brothers, of course, become interested in you only when they observe that your light is shining brightly. For they know that you are then READY to contact them, and that your motive is pure and that you are reaching upward to them for GREATER LIGHT. Believe me, they are happy to receive you!

Remember, however, that it is far more important for each of us to find the "voice of God" within us, and be guided by that voice than to depend upon any other person or persons. In our upward journey into LIGHT, LOVE and LIBERATION, we are assigned higher Teachers to assist us. Their duty is to aid us in making our own inner connection with the "Diamond Star" --the Soul-Center within our own hearts.

So never lose sight of that purpose. You will enjoy the loving companionship of many wise and noble Teachers as you travel the UPWARD PATH. They will imbue you with a zeal, fervor and enthusiasm you've never before experienced! You will thrill with joy and gratitude, for their light will enable you to carry out your particular job at this time and in the days to come. I tell you it will be THRILLING!

LIGHT IS NOW
INCREASING FOR
OUR SUN SYSTEM
IS ENTERING NEW
REGIONS OF LIGHT

People everywhere on the planet are starting to wake up to a new STIMULUS... Some understand it. Others are still in the "dark" as to its source and meaning. The amazing fact is, our entire solar system with all of its planets, is moving into new and powerful regions of light in God's universe. It is the sign that we are nearing the close of the Old Dispensation and stepping boldly into the NEW ERA. As we do so, the intensity of cosmic light energy is being increased to such a degree that those who are on the side of LIGHT will express constantly greater light and "inner knowing".

In fact, sincere New Age souls will SHINE with light, so that their very bodies and garments will radiate MORE LIGHT. But those who are on the side of the "goats" will become ever darker and darker in their desires and ideals. I believe I can give you an example of this condition right now. Try to find a bright, cheery, light-colored suit of clothes in a department store nowadays. It's almost impossible. Everything is such a dark, sombre color. The "Continental Look" is the latest fashion now, for men and women. They're bringing it over here from Europe. For many people it will be just the thing. For me...no thanks! I still prefer the lighter colors. They symbolize the Light. They uplift. This is, we all know, the time of cosmic light. The time when great light should illumine and beam from all of us! Especially in America.

The karmic history of Europe is by no means good. The continent is in certain portions quite decidedly "Old Age". Our friend Edgar Cayce gave one of his remarkable psychic readings in 1934 in which he said: "The upper portion of Europe will be CHANGED in the twinkling of an eye.."

As the great light gradually increases there is greater contrast between those "in the light" and those enmeshed in materiality. So do not be alarmed if you are misunderstood by the multitudes (and your relatives). They have not awakened.

We are aware -- you and I -- that NOW is the time for a great INWARD PREPARING. That is why we have been gathered together with one united purpose. To CONTACT THE LIGHT. To get ourselves attuned -- our mental television sets activated -- so that we are enabled to know and commune with the Guiding Minds of the spiritually advanced Teachers.

We live in a great time. There is a great and glorious destiny just ahead for all true New Age individuals. We are going to realize that glorious destiny...mark my words. All of us Sons and Daughters of Light, in one strong and united body, are moving onward, upward and Godward. And as we move upward under the higher direction of the Brothers and our own High Self intelligence (which gives us an open line direct to our Creator God) we become MIGHTY TORCHES OF ASSISTANCE!

Your flame of LIGHT will become so bright that it will enlighten and assist a countless number of "New Age souls" who are only waiting for your light to uplift them. But it is also your divine responsibility, as a New-Age Individual, to _maintain inner poise and control_ in all of the higher activities you engage in. Poise, control and balance must be your guideposts now more than ever. _Find your own center of Christ-Balance within yourself first._ Then reach upward to commune with the higher beings. Express always in love from your Soul-Center. That will keep you balanced and harmonious at all times.

Guard against emotional imbalance, for over-excitability hinders clear thinking. Develop a deep inner calm and peace, for that is your assurance of protection from the Wise Ones. Walk this Path, reach UPWARD in thought and love, and you too will know the MAGIC of higher contact. Then, with this Wisdom, all the Powers of Light will walk with you!!

SECRETS OF HIGHER CONTACT

Part Three

Contacting Your Secret X

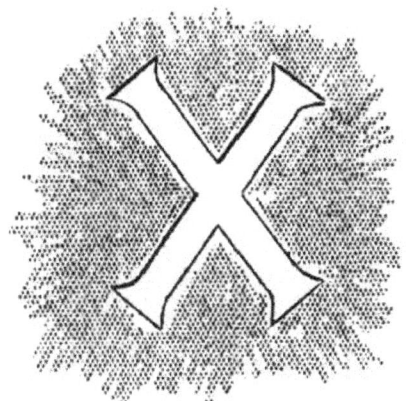

The first step to take on the wonderful path that leads to "Higher Contact" with our Space Brothers is this: making "X" contact. It is so important to all who are desirous of consciously communicating with those inhabitants of other worlds, that I cannot over-emphasize it.

What is "X"? Simply a symbol for your own highest spirit-self. It is the high-self intelligence of you.

X, as we all know, is used in mathematics to stand for the "unknown factor". The unknown factor in my own life for many long and bewildering years was my Higher Self. I was like countless other persons on our planet, totally unaware of the existence of my high self. It is exceedingly difficult -- if not impossible -- to become aware of one's higher self when one's ordinary human self demands all the attention.

In 1940 I had a most unusual and startling experience which brought me "face to face" with my unknown higher self. I had never, previous to this time, had any kind of contact with a living Master or Teacher from another planet. I was, however, a deep and serious student of the "hidden secrets" of life. My bookshelf bulged with "occult" books of every description--- and yet -- I had never touched reality.

One night after reading a chapter or two of an advanced and complicated treatise dealing with "White Magic", I turned out the light in my bedroom and went to sleep. It was my usual bedtime -- ten o'clock -- and sleep came quickly.

I slept for several hours. Then, at about 2:00 A.M., I suddenly was aroused to full conscious awareness. Something strange and unusual was about to happen. I sensed that what was about to occur would be of deep soul significance. In a few moments my premonition was confirmed.

As I lay there on my bed in the darkness of my little room, opening both eyes to see whatever I could in the dark, it happened. A tall, graceful being in the form of a man wearing a light flowing robe, quietly entered through the closed door and walked over to my bedside. Yes, he had walked right through the solid door and as he stood beside me, I felt my own body begin to tremble. My eyes seemed riveted upon the remarkable being who had just "stepped into" my life in this unusual manner.

He was indeed extraordinary. Tall, well proportioned and majestic in his appearance, I had only to look into those amazing eyes of his to know. Here was a being of marvelous power and intelligence. His entire body radiated a beautiful light so that I could see him easily in the dark. It seemed to me that little rays of light shone from his large eyes which sparkled like blue diamonds. The calm expression on his face indicated perfect balance of strength and love and high intelligence. And yet -- I was excited and afraid.

Why? I do not know. Perhaps fear comes too naturally, too easily to the majority of us earthlings. Maybe that is why we get into fights and yes, wars so frequently. For me, in those early days, fear was an emotion I had not yet cast out of my consciousness. I felt that emotion then.

The tall Master -- for such he most certainly was -- had no intention of disturbing me further. At once he became aware of my fear and with a gentle, understanding smile upon his lips, turned around and was soon gone.

Then came the voice of my own Higher Self -- soft but clear -- "Be not fearful of your Teachers. Learn the lesson of higher love. See harmony within all creation and build a greater realization of oneness with all living beings. In this perfect love all fear is dissolved."

That was a big lesson for me to learn. And it was not until I had really transmuted fear into the higher love that the "Brothers of the Higher Arc" could reach me and teach me other important lessons. Keep this in mind as you continue your progress as a New Age Individual seeking higher contact. Love is the realization of oneness. It is the soul's sincere desire for health, harmony and happiness within all beings.

Don't, for heaven's sake, be like me -- so upset that I actually "frightened" my teacher away! When your time for meeting a marvelous being from Venus, arrives, by all means try to maintain your composure. There is no good reason to be afraid of any advanced human being who sends out the wonderful vibration of higher love to you. On the other hand, if the "harmony vibration" is missing in your contact with any being of advanced intelligence, be careful. It is possible for us earthlings to contact advanced beings who are advanced mentally but not spiritually. My advice is to always be wary of any intelligence who is "all mind, but no heart". There are such, contacting earthlings, but these are not to your highest welfare.

It is your privilege and responsibility to "test the teachers" before following their suggestions or advice. How do you test them? Very simply. By the trinity principles of Power, Love and Wisdom. Our Brothers of the Higher Arc -- especially those from Venus -- always bring about a beautiful and "balanced" effect when they communicate with you. That is because they never over-emphasize one aspect of the trinity at the expense of the other two. When they apply Power they use an equal amount of Love and Wisdom at the same time.

This causes their thoughts, feelings and actions to be harmonious, positive and joyously constructive. No matter what Teacher you contact, either on the mental, the astral, or the physical plane, test him or her for BALANCE. If you sense inwardly that he is bringing inharmony into your soul by an imbalanced vibration, he is NOT your true Teacher.

Regarding all contacts with the Brothers, a word or two of caution. Never be frivolous. Frivolity is out of place, because it indicates disrespect. Communication with higher beings from advanced worlds is serious and of the deepest importance to you and humanity. Reaching the mind of a Space Brother from Venus, for example, is no simple matter. There has to be a very close "attunement" of both soul and mind before the condition of rapport is achieved between you.

Here is the basic procedure to follow:

1. Whole-hearted desire. You must desire to contact the Brothers of the Higher Arc, with a deep-souled intensity.

2. Belief in them. You must feel in your heart that the Brothers exist just as you do; that they can respond to you.

3. Be Sincere with yourself. Ask yourself, "Why do I desire to contact the Space People?" Purity of motive and Sincerity are the attitudes which will protect you from unwanted, lower entities and vibrations. They are your "shield and buckler".

4. Raise your vibrations. Body, Soul, Spirit have to be raised to a new and higher level of awareness. Your awareness must rise above earth's sphere until it reaches the High Arc of Venus or other advanced realm of human life.

I have learned that the Venusians, and all of the many other higher beings, are in close touch with their own "X" or Higher Self. They are "in tune" with its BALANCED-LIGHT principle. This is the balancing and illuminating factor from which comes all wisdom. And that is why Earthlings who desire to know and serve the Brothers, should practice identifying themselves with their High Self ("X") first. By doing this and by not identifying yourself with your desires, or your emotions, a great change will take place in you. No longer will you feel yourself to be an insecure, limited human personality. You have changed your identity. Of your own free choice you have accepted the "X" (higher self) as your true self.

However, this is only the beginning. Your individual soul will not be able to hear the soft, still voice of your higher self until you have first slain the Dragon of Desire. This does not mean that you should "kill out all desires". Not at all. It does mean that you must not permit yourself to be so tossed upon the stormy sea of emotions, passions, appetites and personal desires that the beautiful voice of your higher self cannot reach your ears.

To contact your Secret "X", it is essential to bring more tranquillity, more balance and more self-control into all thoughts feelings and actions. Here is how to do this. As you go about your daily activities, no matter where you may be or what you might be doing, think of your Secret X. Think of it as a perfect blend of Light, Love and Life. Or if you prefer, as Intelligence, Harmony and Power. A balanced trinity. Think of it with joy.

When your trinity of Power, Harmony and Intelligence are blended in your consciousness so that they become one unit, that is when you may reach your Higher Self. Then it is that you may hear the voice of your own immortal spirit whispering within your soul. Practice listening at least once daily for that voice of your own "X". Early morning is the very best time to contact it. The moment you waken from your night's sleep, listen quietly in silence and calmness for some message from your higher self. Learn to commune with that high source.

The Space People -- Brothers of the Higher Arc -- have long since learned to live and think and express from their Secret "X". To them there is nothing mysterious, nothing difficult about this. They recognize it to be simply a "unified consciousness" composed of the three higher principles. Namely, Intelligence, Harmony and Power in balance. They say there is indeed a "Shining Presence" within each one of us, regardless of whether we happen to be Earthlings, Venusians, Mercurians, Martians, Jupiterians, Saturnians, or so forth, ad infinitum.

The "Shining Presence", they say, is the glorious result of our consciously blending the triad of Intelligence, Harmony and Power into a more complete and perfect Self. Because the inhabitants of Venus and other advanced worlds have discovered the magic of their own Secret "X" and attune all of their thoughts, feelings and actions to its harmony vibration, you will find that the most effective way for you to communicate with them will be to attune first to your Secret "X". Thus affinity will exist.

SECRETS OF HIGHER CONTACT

Part Four

How To Uplift Others Now

The Venusians say that Higher Love is the keynote of the coming New Age. Why? Because Higher Love seeks Balance and Balance is the great secret of Harmony, Peace, Health and all Wisdom. This higher love is different from earthly love.

Earthly love is important. But it is so often binding us instead of releasing us into greater freedom. The reason it does so is because it generally lacks the "balance" factor, and is based more upon self-getting than self-giving.

Higher love frees, releases, harmonizes everything it contacts. It is not "possessive" nor restrictive. Rather it brings you a realization of "oneness" and a joyous, harmonious freedom that makes your heart sing in gratitude. When you come into this happy feeling it is like warm sunshine beaming down upon you from above. You feel its gentle rays and want to bask in that sunshine of Higher Love forever.

When man on our planet comes into an understanding of this higher love -- to the point where he desires harmony, health and happiness within all creation -- then he will be ready to reach out to Venus and other worlds and extend the hand of love to them. The Lord Thinkers of Venus will then welcome and embrace us openly. But you know as well as I do that the highly spiritualized minds on advanced planets are not going to stand for any childish attempts by earthment to "conquer" outer space through brute force. No indeed.

The Lords and Teachers of Venus are very wise. War and violence have long since been banished from their glorious world. It is the planet of the Christ-Love principle, and they intend to keep it that way. Gently but firmly they tell us that a realization of higher love is essential before the "astronauts" of earth will really master interplanetary flight. Until we are willing to extend a hand of love to them, we shall continue to "miss our target" time after time.

The first requisite is to practice giving freely of our higher love vibration. When you desire within your heart and mind and soul to harmonize, unify and uplift any person or situation, you _are_ sending out the right vibration. It is a desire or yearning for a condition of exquisite harmony, wellbeing, and happiness to exist within all living beings. That _is_ higher love. Give freely of it. Expand your love to take in all races all men, women and children on all planets as one great brotherhood. Then we shall all be working together in harmony for the unlimited GOOD of all humanity. As you and I and all New Age souls express more love -- not the self-getting variety, but the freeing love -- all men and nature will work together joyously in Cooperative Brotherhood. This is the way of love. It is the way to uplift others now.

Are you often greatly puzzled as to how you may best assist your friends and loved ones who do not realize these "New Age Truths" the way you do? Here is the answer. You CAN uplift them into a new, higher and happier vibration by doing THREE things for them:

>1. Bless them by recognizing silently that each soul is a center of Light, Love and Life. Mentally project to them an image of themselves as being lifted into a new vibration wherein they see the "Shining Presence" of their own beautiful Higher Self.

>2. Send the clear thought of Peace and Good-Will to those persons you wish to assist. Mentally "spray" their auras with uplifting, pacifying thoughts of peace on earth, Good-Will to all living beings.

>3. Send living energies of color by visualizing these from yourself to those you would help. Colors of the light pink, green, blue, violet, etc. are powerful soul-energizers. Each color has a specific energizing or releasing effect.

These three simple things to do for others will make a definite, constructive change in anybody and everybody involved in this noble activity. Not only do the sender and receiver benefit, but the good vibrations go out to uplift, harmonize and add joy to the entire planet. This will assist all other New Age individuals to make higher contact with their "X" and with the loving souls of Venus. And it will assist you to make contact also, for harmony and balance are the keys to all higher communications. The more who do these, the greater the uplift.

We do not have to use our mental or will-force to tell a person to "do this" or "do that", but just simply send out to him or her the positive vibrations of Peace and Love. And bless that person so he will become aware of his True Self and awaken into a new and wonderful consciousness.

The Space People have clever ways of illustrating their ideas. Once they showed me a picture of a large block of ice in which a fish had been frozen. Nearby was a large axe. Now, how could I release that fish from his prison of ice? My first thought was to grab the axe and chop into the block of ice. "That would be like imposing your will," said my Venusian Mentor. "But what would happen? The axe might cut into the ice so deeply and sharply that the fish would be injured or killed."

Then the answer to the problem was presented. All that I needed to do was to place the block of frozen ice out in the direct sunlight. The sun's warm rays melted the ice and freed the captive fish. No force or violence was required.

To release any person from some negative condition, all you need to do is remember that little lesson of how the fish was freed from its state of suspension. Souls too, get suspended in low vibrations, in discord and illness. They are in a sense frozen in ice, like the fish. While in that negative condition of suspension they cannot make progress. But you and I can help by sending them love. Love melts the ice.

When the ice melts, the soul unfolds and awakens of its own accord. On this planet we are to help one another unfold, and the finest way to do that is by sending out the vibration of love in the color essence of rosy, radiant pink. Tincture the color well with golden light. A dark shade of color is not too helpful. It doesn't give the uplift, and the souls all need this uplift into the higher vibration. Pink color has this uplifting effect. Also, it assists in bringing about a state of well-being and optimism to others. It lifts them up. They begin to see life through "rose-colored glasses" as it were, and this is wonderful, for it sets them free of discordant thoughts.

In sending out this cosmic love vibration, visualize a pure white light pouring down into you from above. See it entering through the top of your head and filling your heart with a golden white radiance. Now visualize that golden white radiance in your heart turning into a golden pink. As soon as you become aware of the pink color, send it out with full power to the one or ones you wish to help. Send it out from your heart center to theirs. See the pink color going out from you and wrapping itself as a radiant mantle around the heart center of another and awakening that heart into a joyous new freedom. This will release them into harmony that will permeate their words and acts.

By sending the high love vibration of this golden pink light to your friends and loved ones, you will be doing them a tremendous service which will help to wipe away a great deal of Karma that you may have accrued through your own past incarnations on this planet Earth. And though you may not at once notice the difference in the appearance or actions of the one you have thus helped, have patience! We have seen this technique succeed time and time again.

SECRETS OF HIGHER CONTACT

Part Five

Will You Be a Contactee?

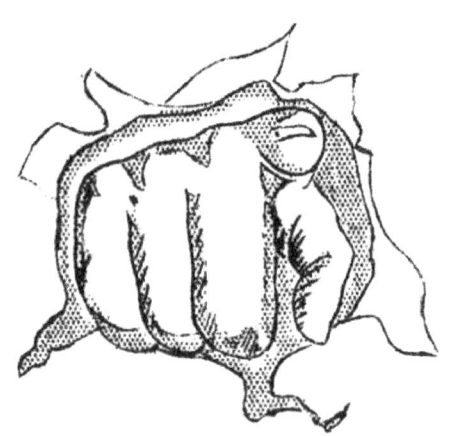

THE ANSWER to that important question is YES. I am quite certain that you -- if you yourself choose to be a Contactee, will become one. How soon depends upon your sincerity of motive and your faithfulness...

Our Space Brothers tell me they desire to make conscious contact with more and more individuals in all walks of life. The reason they desire this is because they have a Great Plan that they are serving... a wonderful Plan, powerful and cosmic and universal in scope.

That Plan is simple in essence, but complex and intricate in its ramifications. The average earthman's mind is not "geared up" to grasp this Cosmic Plan, because as yet we have not advanced to this higher octave of being that our Space Brothers and Sisters have realized. It is so wonderful that they have an earnest desire to contact more and more of the New Age souls that are now awakened.

Now, at the present time on this planet, there are already more than 100,000 awakened souls. The goal, say the Space People, is a minimum of from six to ten million who are fully aware of their presence and purpose here. Since 1944 (three years prior to Kenneth Arnold's sighting) the Brothers of the Higher Arc came in a great host into our atmosphere, to fulfil what they call a fifty year plan in the higher interests of Earth and its people.

With great caution and wisdom, these Brothers did not reveal to any one individual the entire workings of the Plan. One by one they have been contacting the "awakened ones" of earth, and teaching them a certain part of this wonderful Plan of theirs. Bit by bit the pieces have been gathered together, until now at last it is shaping up and we can see the great overall picture much more clearly for the first time. Not even the Contactees knew the vast scope of this Great Plan, but now the complete picture is being released. The Plan is so big it requires a great dedication of each New Age soul to tell others, so that we can uplift more of humanity...into a new octave of vibration. That is the goal. You will find a few clues in your seventh chapter of the Book of Revelation. And if you think there are only 144,000 "saved" souls, read the second half of that chapter!

The Creator has a mighty Plan. The Higher Brothers are consciously cooperating with that Plan, just as you and I may do when we become more aware of it. The Plan includes not only our planet Earth, but all of the Planets in our Solar System. It is a Lift, an uplift in the vibratory frequency of this entire Solar System. It is a Cosmic Upgrading of the Planets and their inhabitants. And although the big change may come suddenly, Nature is leading up to it very gradually, just as she does in all her work. There is a period of growth and preparation and finally the "fruition". We are now approaching that time of fruition.

That is why souls on earth are awakening now. Never before in history have more people begun to LOOK UP to the wise beings from other worlds for guidance and instruction. We realize -- you, I and many others -- that something BIG is impending... something of COSMIC MAGNITUDE. Something that touches each and every one of us deeply, whether the laggard souls accept it or not.

That's why you yearn for Higher Contact. You are seeking actual connection and attunement with the Creator's Plan. You wish to align yourself with that Great Plan and with the Higher Brothers because they are themselves aligned with it.

The way is simple, easy and without force. It is simply a beautiful blending of the principles of Intelligence, Love and Power in a beautiful harmony. This is the real key to Higher Contact, because you see, Higher Contact is just that. You are stepping up into a wonderful NEW vibration -- a higher Dimensional state. A Dimension that will thrill you to the very depths of your soul when you attune harmoniously.

This thing is Master-Minded. Each awakened soul -- and we said that there are about 100,000 now -- has a special role to play in this mighty New Age drama. It is principally the job of awakening and harmonizing other souls. But no two of us will serve in the same capacity. Each will have his or her own unique manner of serving the Big Plan, so there will be practically no duplication of roles.

As more of us find our place in this activity -- and no New Age individual is happy until he does -- we will start to raise the "mass consciousness" in a wonderful way. The awareness of the masses of people on this planet will be stepped up, and this, our Brothers say, is the way it will be.

We will not ALL be awakened, but millions of us will be. Millions of us will be "Contactees". You very likely shall be one of these, secure, loving and enlightened by the Brothers. You'll be centered and poised in the mightiest principle of ALL. The mighty principle of the BALANCED LIGHT. That is the beautiful balance of Love, Power and Wisdom within YOU.

Are you ready for Higher Contact? Yes, <u>if</u> you yourself are certain that your reason, your motive for contacting the Space Brothers is pure. <u>Purity of motive</u> is most important and this means simply that <u>you are not</u> seeking to contact the Brothers merely to satisfy a curiosity. Curiosity-seekers are really selfish souls who are more interested in their own little personal desires than in serving the Great Plan. <u>Any self seeking motive keeps one's soul-vibration in too low an octave of vibration.</u> That hinders all higher communications.

Therefore, clarify your real motive first of all. With purity of motive (serving the highest Universal Will and Purpose) you then should devote 5 minutes in the morning, 5 minutes at noon, and 5 minutes at night to conscious recognition of your own "X" or Higher Self. The Higher Self dwells on a plane above your Human Personality and is always attuned to the CHRIST-BALANCE LIGHT in the universe. And here is the SECRET. The more of that BALANCE-LIGHT you receive from your Higher Self, the more perfectly balanced you will be in body, mind and soul. With <u>balance</u> you are much better able to carry on a most intelligent and perfectly rational conversation with the Space People, who are highly advanced mentally and spiritually.

<u>VERY IMPORTANT</u>: Call for the BALANCE-LIGHT every time you think of your secret "X". <u>Ask that the light be sent down from the high self into your brain and into your heart center.</u> This marvelous practice clears your mental "channels" for communications via Telethot (telepathy) from the Brothers.

The Space Brothers do want each and every one of you to BE a Contactee. They are confident that you CAN become one. This is in the Great Plan you know. It is high time, they say, that earthman awakens from his dream and connects to REALITY. The Balance-Light is tremendously real. Our Space Brothers and Sisters are real. So are their Celestial Ships in our skies.

A Contactee must anchor himself to realities at all costs. To follow the siren call of fantasy, imagination and make-believe will only result in self-delusion and imbalance. Before we reach for contact, we seek first the Balance Light. And <u>the more that Light of your "X" is invoked and welcomed into your body as outlined in this book, the more perfectly balanced you become.</u> Then as you reach up to make the thought communications with the High Beings, you work in harmony and poise. There is no imbalance of mind. It becomes, in fact, <u>better</u> balanced.

Becoming a Contactee is your New Age privilege. Now is the time to apply these secrets given you for your higher progress. If you will invoke the Light as directed, if you will use great zeal in carrying out instructions, you WILL BE A CONTACTEE.

SECRETS OF HIGHER CONTACT

Part Six

Your Most Important Role

You have played many important roles in your past lives upon planet earth, but your biggest role is just ahead. In simple words, it is this: You -- as an awakened New Age soul -- are needed to assist in the <u>liberation</u> of this planet.

More than 100,000 men, women and children in all walks of life, of all age groups, are now beginning to "liberate" those around them...and the ranks of our mighty Army of Love, Life, and Light is growing by leaps and bounds!

You belong to this New Age Army of Light. You, dear friend, are one of the Liberators of mankind. What are your important duties? To Balance, Harmonize and Interpret the present and coming events in the light of your New Age knowledge!

Of course there are many key figures in this movement. In the foreground among the Flying Saucer enthusiasts are the Contactees -- those men and women who have made mental or astral or physical contact with Spacemasters from far distant planets. Most of these Contactees have written books telling about their amazing experiences. They also lecture before the various Flying Saucer Clubs and New Age organizations.

I have -- as one among many Contactees -- received vital thought communications from the Space People. I have told of my various contacts from the public lecture platform in many cities here in California. Book after book has come forth from my typewriter, in accord with the wishes of the Space Brothers. But I say to you now...heart to heart and soul to soul...it is not the writing of books nor the lecturing that is most important in the liberating, the freeing of humanity.

In your New Age service, you <u>may</u> write or lecture. But those are to be secondary activities. Getting in touch with the Space Brothers comes first, and this means you must qualify for communication. Prepare yourself to be a crystal-clear channel for their messages and directives. Then, when they contact your mind and soul, there will not be interference from your Lesser Self which would confuse their message.

Not everybody can qualify as an author or public speaker, and the Brothers say that is not the main issue anyway. The big thing to do right now, individually, is to consciously and voluntarily ALIGN OURSELVES with the Great Purpose of our Creator. "Tuning-in" on that purpose is our prime objective.

Now, I have good news for you. Due to the upliftment of the thoughts, feelings and actions of all of you during the past few months, much negativity that would otherwise have manifested on this planet has been to a great extent nullified. We are making headway. The positive Balance Principle of Inner Harmony is being anchored in every city, large and small, of EVERY STATE in the U.S.A. Inner harmony creates Outer harmony.

We desire harmony. Why? Because we know great changes are imminent. We must have the Balance-Principle well anchored in our minds and hearts in order to hold the balance in the days ahead. Our individual efforts to do this are most effective.

We know that a great cold spell just recently went through our country in the midwest and Great Lake areas. Chicago staggered under a siege of cold that hit 30° below. People died there through the intense cold. Climate everywhere has been changing considerably in the past few years...more than we've ever noticed in previous times. One man said to me when the weather in California was very hot, unseasonably, that it seemed like Heaven "with Hell just around the corner!" Something sinister impending.

The truth is, it is not at all sinister, but COSMIC. And none of us need have any fear whatsoever of these changes. "When ye see these things come to pass, lift up your head and rejoice, for your redemption draweth nigh." This is what Jesus told His elect. Who are the elect? Those who elect (choose) to AWAKEN. Our Brothers keep telling us over and over again that Higher Love -- the Christ-Balance Principle -- casts out all fear. It harmonizes the environmental conditions and keeps you protected.

That's why many awakened souls are sending out this Love Blessing -- not the sickly, sentimental love that is generated by weaklings -- but a powerful, balancing and unifying energy that, if need be, could SAVE A CITY. Multiply that immortal "New Age Energy" by several million and it can actually SAVE A WORLD... This is your NEW AGE ACTIVITY.

These are your instructions: Anchor the Light, the Balance Principle in your heart and mind firmly. Hold the personality or human self OPEN always to any inflow of power, light or wisdom from your Higher Self. Free your physical body and your etheric body of any impurity, shadow, cloud or obstruction to the Light. Each of us must cleanse our bodily vehicles of impurities so that the Light can flow freely into us without resistance and without causing pain. Let New Joy replace old shadows!

Act One of the great world drama began with the awakening of humanity to the fact that interplanetary beings exist. Act Two -- world liberation -- now begins and YOU are needed!

SECRETS OF HIGHER CONTACT

Part Seven

Space Brothers Need YOU Now!

Yes, a totally new and marvelous phase of the Great Plan --which the Brothers themselves know and serve -- is now beginning to unfold. It is WORLD LIBERATION. It is the second act in the mighty drama that involves every one of us.

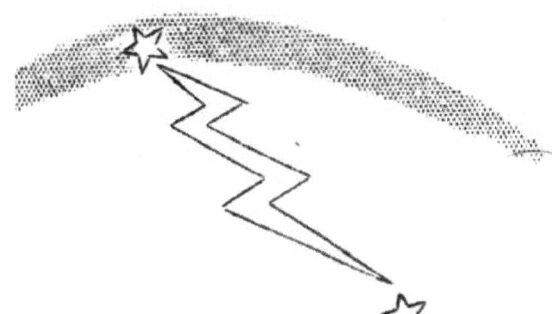

You are needed to assist the Space People in liberating mankind from its hopeless burden of negative "Karma". Here is what they desire you do do now!

(1) <u>Condition yourself now for conscious contact, mind-to-mind, with the Venusians and other Brothers of the Higher Arc</u>. Do this by purifying your MOTIVE first of all. In purity of motive is the GREAT SECRET of making Higher Contact. And the purest motive is simply this: To follow in perfect accord with the Plan of that Great Being we call our Creator. He has it all figured out. And that Plan is coming down from high spiritual sources through the great Balance-Light. It is the purest white Light known and we call it the Christ-Balance Light.

As your innermost motive then attunes with the motive of the Creator, your light expands. And as it expands, the Brothers will become aware of it and will then come to you to assist you. At first they will guide you gently, without your knowing it, perhaps. Later, as you grow stronger and more valuable to the cause you will be contacted telepathically and receive instruction and "working orders" direct from the Brothers themselves.

(2) Of your own free choice -- never because of what I or anyone else says -- <u>begin to adopt a more vital, natural, and meatless diet</u>. How and what you eat will affect your ability to "tune-in" with the Space Brothers. You can raise or lower your personal vibrations by the kinds of food you put into your stomach. Here is what happens: <u>The eating of meat or flesh foods causes a dark shadow or cloud to form upon the etheric body</u>. The etheric body is the pattern or sustaining vehicle upon which the physical body is built. A person with clairvoyant vision can at on once perceive the dark cloud that forms on the inner body when one eats meat. This cloud acts as an interference or obstruction to the Balance-Light that is sent down from the High Self. Unless the Light from your High Self can get through easily, your vibra-

tion remains too low in intensity for clear and easy communication with the minds of the Space People.

As you gradually make the required change in your diet, replacing fish, fowl and flesh with protein from non-toxic sources such as almonds, sunflower seeds and other vitalized foods..and open yourself to the inflow of Light...the cloud that may now be obstructing your Higher Contact will start to dissolve. Now I myself found that until I did change my diet, thereby raising my vibrations, I was unable to make Higher Contact even though I had a great desire to do so.

But to make any changes in diet -- or even in your own thinking -- without having the urge to do so coming from within your own self; of your own free choice, is apt to produce conflict. And you can never go two ways at the same time successfully. It tears you apart. I realize that many would-be Contactees as well as you who may already be Contactees, have a certain amount of conflict within yourselves. The Brothers are asking you to go in one direction and your personal will is tugging at you to go in the opposite direction.

This situation must be resolved without conflict. When we begin to embrace the Great Purpose of the Guiding Mind that brought us into being -- and that directs the Cosmos -- then the conflict of the small-self-will dissolves.

You will find this: That if you will make the effort to set aside the small-self-will and reach up for this greater Light, Love and Power coming now from the Creator, an amazing thing will happen. The Space Brothers, who give the details of this Great Plan to New Age individuals, will help you to "connect up" with the Light of your High Self. It will then become easier and easier for you to set aside your little will for something far, far grander and nobler. You will find one day, that the smaller will has "melted" or submerged itself INTO the Greater Will!

Then, as more Light pours into your brain and higher centers (pituitary and pineal glands) you will notice a wonderful new mental clarity. The thoughts of the highly intelligent beings of Venus and other advanced worlds will then come into your consciousness clearly.

(3) When your light shines brighter you will be seen by the "Brothers of the Higher Arc". One of them -- your present Teacher on your individual ray -- will get in touch with you telepathically. This will happen only at the proper time. When it occurs, do not be startled nor alarmed. It is most important for you to observe the following practice. Obtain for yourself at least one (two would be better) psychic gems or stones. You will use them to assist you in raising your vibrations sufficiently high to

enable you to project your thoughts, and commune with our marvelous Space Brothers.

The Gem Exchange, Bayfield, Colorado will send you a complete list of recommended psychic stones for this purpose. A postcard to Mr. S. N. Green, Owner of the Gem Exchange at Bayfield, Colorado will bring you a quick reply and details about the "Telolith" Stone which I fully endorse.

It is essential that all psychic gems, crystals, etc. be first "purified" of any mixed magnetisms of low vibration and then spiritually "charged" with a high potency Light from the High Self. The crystal or psychic stone then becomes imbued with the Balance-Light vibration of the spiritual self. This is a powerful aid to contacting our Space Brothers, since the "charged" stone steps up your capacity to receive as well as transmit thoughts. All that is necessary is to place the charged stone upon the head so that it is directly over the pituitary gland. Unless a psychic stone is properly de-magnetized and charged with the Light power from the High Self, it is not fully effective for Higher Contact. (See Venusian Secret Science, end pages.)

(4) Set aside a regular time for Higher Communication. It is preferable to have this "Contact Time" just after you rise in the morning, and before breakfast. It should always be at the same time each day and in the same room. Now, at the exact time you have chosen, sit down at your desk or table with pen and pad ready. Hold your pen so that only penpoint is lightly touching the paper -- no part of hand or arm should touch. Your objective is to contact your Cosmic Teacher mentally during the next 15 minutes. When contact is made, he will use your arm to write his name first. (Let the pen move freely of its own accord. You may sense a kind of electric impulse prompting movement in your arm.) If the name is slow in coming, mentally request your Cosmic teacher to give you the name he wishes to be known by. He will do so if you have qualified for communication with him, by the new brightness of your own light. And he may also identify himself to you by means of a special symbol uniquely his own. As an actual example, my present Mentor uses the name Ramel and identifies himself by the sign of the Golden Ram. With the sign comes an individual vibration which no other being can duplicate, for no two beings have the same vibration, as all of them (and us) are individuals with different soul and spirit patterns.

Your teacher will identify himself clearly and positively at the first successful "Contact Time". At the end of your contact, say that you are ready to discontinue if agreeable with the Teacher. Wait until he signs off by giving his name, before you leave. This "sign-off" procedure is important and must not be neglected. It insures against the entrance of possible lower entities at this point. We are not endorsing "automatic writing" as such, and later on, your teacher may not need to write thru your hand, but will communicate entirely by telethot. You will know when to discontinue the "writing" because you will begin to get more and more of your teacher's inspirational words or ideas, or even "picture-thoughts" which you will be able to recognize as coming from your teacher. So the writing may stop.

But you will use your regular time for Higher Communication. And you may continue using the Telolith and other psychic "aids". When using the Telolith, do not try to hold the stone in place with your hand. Either "tape" it to your forehead between the eyes or place it on top of the head, using a lightweight cap over the stone to keep it in place while you are concentrating on the communication. Next, mentally surround yourself with a golden white light. Visualize it pouring down from above into your entire body and immersing you in a great Tube of Light. This is your protection against undesired low vibrations.

Your Venusian Insignia (for details see list at back of this book) should be in sight in the room where you communicate daily. Now, put your full attention upon the Venusian Insignia for a full five minutes. As you gaze quietly at the tiny spot of pure white at the center of the Insignia, centering your attention upon the white spot, soon the muscles of your eyes will relax slightly. You are inducing a condition known as the Subliminal state of awareness. In this condition you will become more sensitive to the thought energies of the Space Brothers. So the Venusian Insignia is a true contacting device, having the advantage of being a definite physical object. Therefore it is a better "attuning link" than a mental image, for most persons. All physical aids can be dispensed with later, but not until your "attunement" has been well established.

After gazing quietly at the Insignia for five minutes, close your eyes and slowly count to seven. With each count, mentally request your consciousness to rise higher and higher. Without this "stepping stone" stepping-up process, mental contact is much more difficult to achieve. After mental contact has been achieved and the teacher has "signed off" by giving his name, begin counting IN REVERSE from seven back down to ONE, slowly. Then with open eyes, stamp your foot once on the floor to assert symbolically that you have returned to normal state of consciousness. Under no circumstances should you neglect this!

These are the secret techniques you have been waiting for. Put them to work for you at once. Do not feel discouraged if you fail to make contact immediately. It merely means that you must continue invoking the Light and raising your body vibrations, in your daily life. Like any other reward in life, Higher Contact must be earned. THOUGHT, FEELING and ACTION always working together harmoniously and in balance at the highest level will prepare you for this great experience. I urge you to reach up! Now! For the Higher Brothers are calling you.

"THE COSMIC QUESTION BOX"

By MICHAEL X

Q.1. How soon will I be contacted by the Saucer People?

A. This depends upon you. Our Space Brothers are making mental contacts now with those individuals who are in advance of the majority of the people. You can earn your contact by following directions carefully. In time ALL New Age individuals will be contacted.

Q-2. Is two-way telepathic communication with the intelligent beings of other planets possible?

A. Not only is it possible, "Contactees" in all parts of the world are doing it. At present time, most of this Telethot communication is done at a relatively short distance between the spacecraft in our atmosphere and us on earth.

Q-3. What are the benefits of contact with Space People?

A. Tremendous new mind and soul freedom through contact with powerful and advanced intelligences..beings who have actually connected up with the big universal realities!

Q-4. Can every sincere individual become a Contactee?

A. Sincerity is very important. However, purity of one's motive is the biggest determining factor. Our Space Brothers know they can accomplish their good purpose only by carefully choosing those who are mature enough in soul to be loyal and dedicated cooperators in the Great Plan.

Q-5. Will my Space Teacher communicate with me in English?

A. He will communicate in whatever language is most familiar to you.

Q-6. Are there many different types of Space People?

A. (1) Physical beings whose vibratory frequency is considerably higher than ours, (2) Etheric beings who dwell in the etheric regions around the earth and around other planets, (3) Celestial beings involved in the cause side of creation (Angelic Beings.) The first two classifications are made up of our Elder Brothers and Sisters who have already advanced to the next "Hier Arc" of Soul, mind and Body progress. They make use of Spaceships, Space Stations and mental contact methods.

Q.7. Does life on Venus resemble our life on Earth?
A. Yes, but more spiritual, more perfect, more glorious.

Q-8. How may I be sure it is really my Space Teacher who is in contact with me telepathically, and not my own mind speaking to me?

A. First, you will notice a rapid delivery of ideas to you when a Brother of the Higher Arc is in contact with you. Your own mind is not generally as definite and swift in its functioning. Second, the knowledge your Space Teacher gives you will be completely unlike anything you are now aware of

Q-9. How can I protect myself against lower intelligences, for example, beings from the lower astral planes?

A. Like attracts like in the mental realms. If you keep your physical, mental and soul vibrations high through high thought, high feeling and high deed...your aura and mental wavelength instantly repels and wards them off. It is up to you whom you will commune with, just as it is up to you to make the decision as to which associates you prefer. Purity of motive protects you best, because it permits more powerful Light from the High Self to flow into your body. Low entities cannot tolerate the higher vibration of that Light.

Q-10. Why are the Space Brothers contacting us?

A. For World Liberation. They are cleaning the astral realms inside and outside of our earth, and freeing our minds of "Old Age" concepts. This new and higher phase of their work -- contacting as many of us as possible -- is in line with their purpose of preparing this planet and our people for the coming "Initiation in Light".

Q-11. Why is it that the good has such little effect on the bad in our world? Why is there so much wrong on earth?

A. Because earthman -- generally speaking -- has not yet accepted voluntarily the Christ-Balance way of life. Man does not consciously recognize the importance of keeping harmony within all nature. His own soul is asleep to the universal realities of limitless LIFE, LOVE and LIGHT all around as well as within himself and in _all_ of creation.

Simply put, Man has ignored the God-Plan of Higher Love. In its place earthman has substituted his own egotism and personal will to dominate and conquer all creation -- including outer space -- by mental cunning and sheer physical might. He has thereby greatly imbalanced his thoughts, feelings, and actions. Most men -- our leaders in high places included -- see only the outer, material appearances of things. It is the small minority of wise humanity who are now aware of inner realities or "soul" purpose within all things. We must hold the balance.

Release Your Cosmic Power

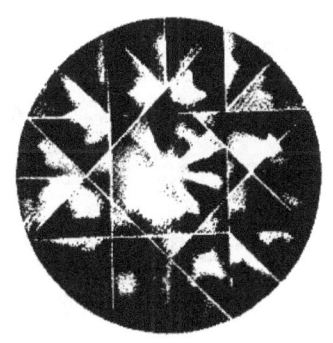

by

Michael X

RELEASE YOUR COSMIC POWER

- by -

MICHAEL X

* * *

This is an Educational and Inspirational Course of Study...especially written and intended for NEW AGE Individuals everywhere. The following Seven Sections are contained herein:

1. "CHAOS AHEAD FOR THE MASSES!"

2. "HOW IS YOUR COSMIC BALANCE?"

3. "THE COSMIC BALANCE SECRET"

4. "SOME PROOFS OF THE PUDDING"

5. "EACH ONE REACH ONE -- NOW"

6. "YOUR COSMIC POWER PROGRAM"

7. "RELEASING THE COSMIC POWER"

* * * * * *

Statements in this Course are based on Scientific and Super-Sensory Findings. No claim is made as to what the information cited may do in any given case and the Publishers assume no obligation for opinions expressed or implied herein by the author.

FOREWORD

THIS BOOK rings with urgency! The time for mere words without any action behind them, is past. All of us must now go into positive ACTION.

To assist and guide you in this present time of turmoil and confusion that is now gripping the masses of Mankind on Earth, this book with its unusual message has been written.

YOU will find in these pages a positive new "Way of Life" based on the Cosmic Secret of BALANCE. This Secret is vitally essential to you -- and to your world -- at this time.

MANY NEW AGE KEYS to peace, power and poise in today's mixed-up world are contained herein. All of these ideas, suggestions and practices are simple...yet packed with POWER.

This is a HOW TO book, for the Time for intensely practical instructions has come...and you are needed. As you RELEASE YOUR COSMIC POWER a new joy and freedom will be yours.

Although the masses of humanity on the Earth will make of this planet an Arena for their Mad Scenes...none of the violently destructive actions of others will be able to influence you negatively IF you continue to travel the NEW AGE PATH of SERVICE.

I urge you to be strong in your faith that a Higher Destiny is equalizing the great World Karma, and that he who serves his fellows is guided, protected and strengthened...with a magnificent COSMIC LIFE, LOVE, LIGHT!

MICHAEL X

RELEASE YOUR COSMIC POWER

Part 1

"Chaos Ahead For The Masses!"

No question about it. The "Time of The Terrible Turmoil" -- the upsetting, miserable time spoken of by the great French Seer Nostradamus, and by the prophets of the Holy Bible -- is now upon us.

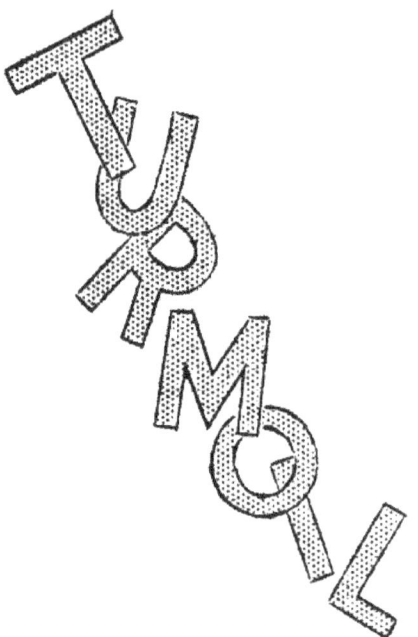

Watch for chaotic times to be the "order of the day" from now on, until this Time of Colossal Confusion passes.

You have sensed it, felt it, realized this fact....a deeply disturbing, chaotic vibration is now taking hold of the masses of mankind. In this book I shall reveal what is really back of this great confusion now gripping the world. And I shall point out a highly effective way whereby you can avoid, side-step, and by-pass the Terrible Turmoil and its dangers.

As I am sitting here at my typewriter clicking out these words that become sentences and and then turn into stimulating ideas, I am thinking strongly of you. You are my New Age Companion, my trusted friend. The fact that you are reading my ideas is proof that we are traveling what we know as the UPWARD PATH together.

YOU then, are my inspiration...my purpose and my reason for writing at all. I could just as easily be doing something else, but that would break my contact with you, and I've come to treasure your friendship even though we may never have met each other.

My friend, we must stick together in these times. All of us "New Age" souls are part of a tremendously important and beloved family. We belong together. Of that I am convinced. For it is up to us to carry the Banner of Life, Love and Light into a "mixed-up" world.

So I am going to talk to you heart-to-heart, and mind-to-mind and soul-to-soul in this book. And you will soon find that we are thinking and acting as one instead of as two separate individuals. But mark this: It is not a weakening but a strengthening condition... our acting as one, because we are unifying our powers into a greater power..and it is a power that <u>acts</u>.

THE GOLDEN LEGION is the name given to that great Legion of souls on earth who believe in Truth and Justice and goodness. It is a mighty power because all of the individual members of the group are unified by right thought, right feeling and right ACTION.

You and I and all the other magnificent members of Earth's GOLDEN LEGION of awakened souls are now "on the march!" Our purpose? To RELEASE OUR COSMIC POWER now for the betterment of our world and ourselves. I am not one of those fellows who believe that things are destined to happen in just ONE WAY, and that there is nothing we can do about it to help matters.

I believe that our ACTIONS can change a lot of things. I believe that people like us, who are truly dedicated to GOLDEN LEGION ACTIVITY, which is simply activity of a practical, positive kind that uplifts the vibrations of our fellowmen and ourselves, are enabled to tap Godlike powers when we REACH UP FOR THEM.

I am not a fatalist. We CAN make amazing changes in ourselves and in our world environment if we make up our minds to do just that, and then move <u>together</u>.

But let us talk plain "turkey". What is really back of all the mass-minded riots, the inter-racial mistrust, and the crime rise and violence today? That is the first thing we ought to discover in order to properly interpret this Great Turmoil that is "busting out" all around us in every part of the world.

WHY are dozens of opposing factions such as the Communists, anti-Communists, anti-Catholic, anti-Protestants, anti-Jew, anti-Negro and anti-white groups arising now in every city of America? Why is there a great CONFUSION in the minds and hearts of people all over the world? Why is humanity so very bewildered? We must know this -- the why of it all -- so that we will understand what is taking place in this Time.

The explanation for the "Colossal Confusion" we see in our world today is this: There has been a definite rise in vibration in our Solar System. Planet Earth is now absorbing many thousands of times more "Angstrom Units" of light than she previously did. An Angstrom Unit is the term used by scientists to measure the length of light waves. It's a tiny unit of length equal to one hundred-millionth of a centimeter. A centimeter -- according to the Metric Table -- is equal to 0.3937 inches or about 40/100ths of an inch.

In a previous book, "YOUR PART IN THE GREAT PLAN", we told you that the Solar System you and I live in is now receiving a greater vibratory stimulation. We pointed out that this stimulation is a positive one, a form of Cosmic Light energy bombardment from outer space. Its origin? A much larger sun than ours, a Central Sun called Vela (around which our Sun and its planets are orbiting) is sending its energy to us.

The Holy Bible speaks of a "first rain" and a "latter rain". It does not mean, however, that Earth is to be drenched with drops of water from moisture-filled clouds. That kind of "rain" would not be especially noteworthy for it happens quite regularly.

No, the "first rain" really means the first rise in vibratory stimulus that the Earth and all the other planets in this Sun System would experience when the Great Central Sun Vela is close enough to influence us.

This has already happened! We are now -- all of us -- experiencing this faster, stronger, vibration. We have been reacting to it ever since 1960 which was the year when the definite vibrational rise took place.

No man, no woman, no child living on Earth at this time can resist this positive new vibration, for the simple reason that it is "irresistible". It has a frequency far above any material frequencies, hence the Cosmic Vibrations are now affecting ALL LIFE levels upon the Earth and elsewhere in our Solar System.

Many, many individuals are, however, very UPSET by this "NEW AGE" vibration they are feeling now. They cannot understand why they should be so CONFUSED, so utterly "mixed-up" in all their reactions. You and I realize that the "mass-minded" are RESISTING the Light.

Resistance simply means that a person wants to cling to the old set of values -- strictly material values which one can see, taste, touch and hang-onto -- in spite of the scientific fact that Mankind's entire set of values IS RAPIDLY CHANGING!

Materialism -- to those who know -- is becoming obsolete, passe, outmoded. New Age organizations in all parts of the world are pointing out this fact... that "the Old Order passeth away" and has never completely satisfied us..even at its best. Not that we desire or need to turn our backs on the comforts and conveniences of the modern way of life..NO. But in order to live up to the increased demands of a stepped-up vibratory environment, what must we do?

Drop all that is negative. All that contracts, restricts, limits you or me or any man, must GO. "The only sin," said Emerson, "is limitation".

Life, Love and Light are the three great positives that are to be accented from now on. But the masses of humanity do not yet realize this. They have been held back for "lo, these many years" by what? Is it not the organized "Forces of Negative" on our planet?

YES! The "Forces of Negative" are no mystery if we once define who and what they are. The best way I know to do this is by contrasting them with the Forces of Light. Then we can see the basic difference.

	Negative	Positive
1.	Death	Life
2.	Hate	Love
3.	Darkness (Ignorance)	Light (Understanding)

Now you will at once see that the "Negatives" are opposite conditions which manifest whenever and wherever the "Positives" are lacking. We call the Forces of Positive the "Christ System" and the "Negatives" make up what we know as the "anti-Christ System".

The "Anti-Christ System" is built upon the false notion that man is "nothing but a hound-dog" -- a well developed animal. So why not keep people chained in Darkness, hating each other and killing each other? The "Money-Changers" have found this "System" works out most profitably for them, and the greedier they get for money the more Ignorance, Hatred and Death they cause in the world. What a system!

The "Christ System" on the other hand, is not at all based on greed for mere dollars. Instead it is based on a BALANCED GIVING, RECEIVING, and REGIVING.

Its goal is to free men and women into a greater awareness of Life, Love and Light and all the other Positives which automatically follow these basic three. You are not looked upon as a "super-animal" under the "Christ System". You are recognized as being a spiritual expression of God the Creator, and as such are entitled to your freedom to travel the UPWARD PATH.

Now here is the important point. Both of these two world-wide systems, the "Christ-System" and the "Anti-Christ System" are now being intensely stimulated by the influx of Cosmic Light from outer space. This Light -- or ultra-high frequency vibration -- is no respecter of persons. Like rain, it falls upon the just and the unjust alike.

It -- the Cosmic vibration from Vela -- augments or increases the negative or "evil" vibrations in humanity even as it stimulates and increases the positive or "good" vibrations in people everywhere. The "first rain" therefore, has stirred up the evil as well as the good qualities in human beings. This is the reason, then, for the MASS CONFUSION, RIOTING and VIOLENCE that has suddenly "let loose" in the world.

This is the reason why we may expect more CHAOS ahead for the masses of humanity who are under the iron grip of the "worn and weary" Anti-Christ System" but who are not yet strong enough to rise UP and OUT of it. Under the Cosmic Plan now in action in our Solar System, many shall be assisted to avoid all that is now upsetting the unwary.

Your GOLDEN KEYS to use now are three: (1) Balance, (2) Positivity (3) Love. I shall explain how to use each of these keys, as we advance page by page. God's unqualified promise and "guarantee" is this...that no harm will come upon you, no confusion will enter your consciousness, no violence will beset your path now or in days to come IF you will use these keys.

RELEASE YOUR COSMIC POWER

Part 2

"How Is Your Cosmic Balance?"

We have stated that the first GOLDEN KEY to the actual achieving of peace, power and poise during the Time of the Terrible Turmoil on earth is BALANCE. In this chapter my purpose will be to acquaint you with a most important discovery pertaining to the human body.

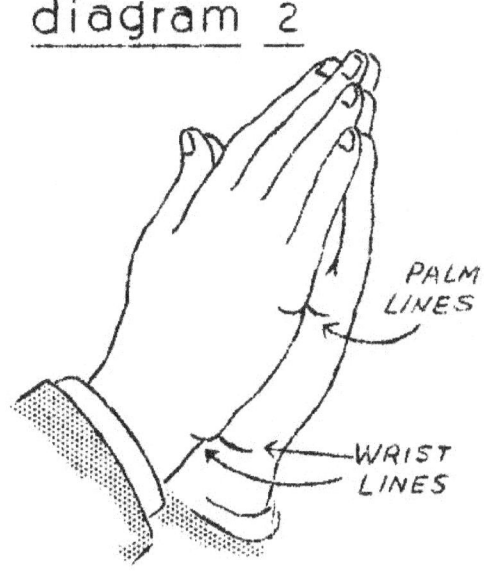

diagram 2

PALM LINES
WRIST LINES

It has long been a common observation by photographers that many of the people who have their picture taken are not in physical "balance". For instance, one eye is quite often higher than the other eye, that is, not "level" with the other eye. Frequently a leg is shorter than the other leg or one shoulder higher than the other shoulder. This is a common complaint of tailors.

When the physical body is carefully measured, it is often found that one arm measures actually much longer than the other arm, or one leg longer than the other leg. Sometimes there is a variance of several inches between the length of the limbs. Why is this so?

Because the physical human body is not at all as "solid" or as "static" as it appears to be. No matter how much of a "heavyweight" you might be physically, your body will -- within certain limits -- shrink or expand instantly depending upon how much or how little the amount of Cosmic Life Force or Cosmic Electricity is permitted to enter into it.

What I am saying is that your physical body is designed by God and Nature to use Cosmic Electricity for its motive force. Every time you take a breath of air your right nostril extracts positive electrons out of that air, and the left nostril extracts negative electrons. This is Cosmic Electricity. Before it is sent into all parts of the body, the "C.E." has to pass through the "Life-Switch" in your brain. It is the purpose of this Life-Switch to send a BALANCED SUPPLY of Cosmic Electricity through your body. If the Life-Switch is not cramped, it sends an equal amount of current into both sides of your body.

BUT if that little Life-Switch -- which is actually the Pituitary Gland -- if it is cramped or depressed in any way, it tends to twist. When twisted, the Life-Switch is unable to send a balanced current into the body. One side of the body -- right or left, depending on how the Life-Switch was cramped, gets a much reduced supply of electricity. This immediately has a detrimental effect on that particular side of the body, shortening that side considerably.

Naturally, that is not good. Whenever the body is allowed to get out of electrical balance we can be sure that the physical body will show distortion.

But that is not the half of it. Body and Mind always "rise and fall" together. We have found that much of what we consider "evil" and "negative" and "destructive" in this world is caused by people who have gotten out of "electrical balance" and remained that way so long their acts became negative...evil.

Fortunately for you and me and all humanity, the principle also works the other way. When people who have been "out of balance" for years are taught the COSMIC BALANCE SECRET and become able to balance themselves, they speedily "eliminate the negative" and begin to make great strides toward constructive living.

THIS, in fact, is the one great HOPE of the world and mankind today. All men must discover BALANCE and when they do we shall have the Millenium of Peace.

Perhaps the greatest revelation in regard to the positive need for human balancing today is this: God made men in a perfect mould, electrically balanced in negative and positive. IF that mould is kept in perfect condition -- balanced -- then all that comes forth from it will be perfect and good. But if we let that balanced would become unbalanced, all that comes forth from it in the way of forms, ideas and acts is bound to be "out of harmony", "destructive" and "negative".

Before I ask you the big question (How is your Cosmic Balance) it is necessary that I explain how we --all of us in the human race -- can and do get out of electrical balance and how we can avoid doing so.

1. Negative Emotions. All negative emotions, particularly hate and fear, cause the brain-case or cranium to tighten and contract upon itself. This causes the Life-Switch (Pituitary) to be cramped and low and twisting. This is one good reason why you should have nothing to do with the "Merchants of Hate" who will be especially active in the Great Turmoil now beginning. Even if you don't join them, refusing to have any part of their hate mongering...they are still dangerous to you and me. Their hate vibrations are filling the ethers of space and the negative vibrations can affect us detrimentally if we are not in balance.

2. More activity of one side of the body. Most of us use the right hand oftener than the left. The "Balance technique" practiced often, can equalize you.

3. Shaking hands. When two right hands meet, the result is harmful to both parties. This is true becausethe right side of the human body is positive and the left side negative, electrically speaking. Imagine what a CLASH occurs when the positive electrons of your right hand contact the positive electrons of my right hand. We are both "shorted out" on the right.

Instead of the CLASH method, let us use the NEW AGE handshake. When you meet a person and wish to shake hands, reach out with your right hand as usual but just before your hands meet gently grasp his right hand close to the wrist with your LEFT hand. Then shake with right hands but keep your left hand on his wrist. Release your right hand first when greeting is over.

TO CHECK yourself now for Cosmic Balance, place your hands together (See Diagram 2), making sure that the lines at the base of your palms are lined up perfectly even with one another. Now put the hands together as if you were praying, and test to see whether one hand is shorter than the other. If so, you are "out of balance". If both hands match in length, you are in good "Cosmic Balance".

RELEASE YOUR COSMIC POWER

Part 3

"The Cosmic Balance Secret"

There is a simple, but highly effective Secret that you should know about at this time. We call it, for want of a better name, "The Cosmic Balance Secret".

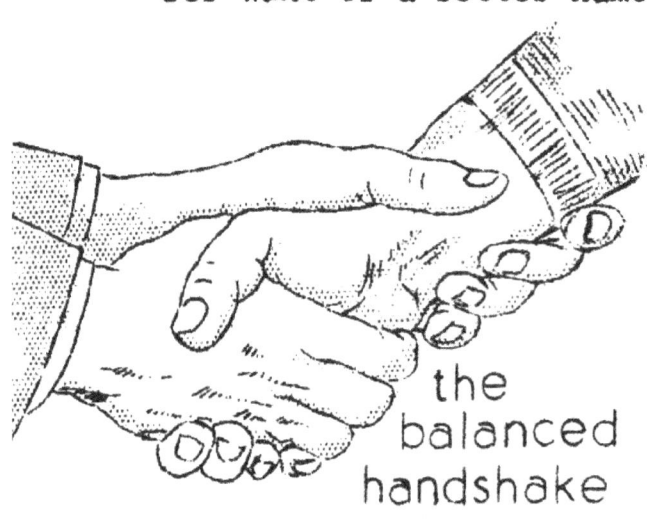
the balanced handshake

Once you have learned this Secret, you'll be able to re-balance yourself in a matter of seconds. By that I mean that you are enabled to restore your "electrical balance" simply by using this Cosmic Balance Secret.

When you use this "NEW AGE" Secret, what happens? Naturally you want to know that before you even decide to make use of the Secret. Of course, I have mentioned briefly some of the good effects you may expect from this technique, but I now wish to assure you that it is a simple and safe procedure. It is not the least dangerous. On the other hand, the good results are worth "shouting" about.

First of all, you have "checked" yourself by putting the two hands together so that the line on your right wrist (at bottom of the palm) exactly matches the natural groove or line on your left wrist. If you found one hand was slightly shorter than the other, it indicates "electrical imbalance" of the body.

What did you find? Were you "in" or "out" of balance? If you are one of the extremely few persons in the world who happen to be "in balance"--good! But in order for you to learn the wonderful technique of re-balancing yourself, it will be necessary for you to let yourself get "out of balance" for a few moments.

Only by first being out of balance, will you be able to see how easily and quickly the Cosmic Balance Secret works when you put it to the "test". So if you are certain that you are "in balance" all you need do to throw yourself out of balance is to shake hands with somebody in the usual way (right to right). Be sure you don't use the NEW AGE handshake for this experiment. Simply shake someone's right hand with your right hand as vigorously as you wish.

After doing that, check yourself for balance again by placing your two hands together in praying position with wrist lines matching. You will now discover that your right hand is not as long as the left hand. Shaking hands right to right has "shorted you electrically" on the right side of the body. If performed just as directed, this experiment is proof of how easy it is to "short-circuit" the body, causing it to become perceptibly "crooked" instead of straight.

You know how politicians are forever shaking the hands of the good people whom they hope will re-elect them? Why, I've seen some of those politicians shake hands with several hundred persons at the end of their political rallys. Imagine, my friend, how "crooked" those politicians must be by the end of the meeting!

All right. You are now ready to learn all about the "Secret" and put it into practice at once. Here is what I am going to ask you to do.

Step 1. Stand or sit relaxed, face looking directly ahead of you.

Step 2. Open your mouth slowly as wide as you comfortably can, in a big "make-believe" yawn. If you wish to cover the mouth with palm of one hand you may do so. It does not matter which hand you use.

Step 3. While mouth is still open wide, lift your eyes upward as high as you comfortably can, as though you were "lifting up your eyes to the mountains, from whence cometh your help". Try to feel an expansion of your forehead above the eyes as you do this. Do not, however, let the head tilt back. Keep your head level, with face pointing straight ahead. Hold this position for 6 seconds, then close mouth, lower eyes to normal position and relax.

You have just performed the "Cosmic Balance Secret" and are now numbered among "those who know". I shall have more to say a bit later as to your vital role in our great cause -- helping the whole world of humanity to know and use this Secret -- but right now the important thing to see is how successful you were in re-balancing your body. At this point, please check yourself for balance in the customary way. How did you do? Are both hands now the same length?

Excellent! Good work! Nine out of ten persons are able to put themselves into perfect balance the very first time they try the Cosmic Balance Secret. I trust you have been successful also. If not, practice the three steps again until you notice the desired results. Also, remember that the real "secret" of this method is to bring about a sufficient "expansion" of the cranium, especially the forehead area.

This expansion -- gentle as it may be -- is very beneficial because it instantly allows more room, more space for the brain and for the little Life-Switch -- Pituitary -- to function. When the skull is cramped, the Life-Switch is also cramped. Practice of the Cosmic Balance Secret acts to "uncramp" the skull bones and this releases the Life-Switch into freer action.

As you lift your eyes upward "to the high hills" you are lifting the cranial bones which in turn lift up the Pituitary Gland, freeing it from its tension and twisted position. It then instantly "untwists" from abnormal cramped position to normal uncramped position. It is then able to send a perfectly balanced supply of electrical current into right, middle, and left sides of the physical body...aligning every cell perfectly from the top of your head to the tips of your toes. All this in a matter of seconds.

Now I have a little story to tell you. It's a true story, and will give you something of the background of the COSMIC BALANCE SECRET...so you will know how the idea came into being and where it started.

Many years ago in a little red schoolhouse, a wise and kindly teacher was giving a talk to the graduation class of very eager, very young students.

"Some of you," said the teacher, "will go out into the world and become skilled workers, such as Carpenters, Machinists, Auto Mechanics, Draftsmen, Stenographers, Secretaries and craftsmen of all kinds.

"And some of you will become professional people such as doctors, lawyers, writers, artists, actors, and other professions of your particular choice. You might even decide to follow my vocation and become a teacher." At this point she smiled broadly.

"All of those vocations and skillful services are needed by humanity and are good, worthy and important pursuits for you to follow in life," she said.

"But there will be a few of you who will go one step beyond those things by discovering some principle -- some universal secret -- that will BLESS THE WHOLE WORLD!"

I do not know how many children in the class that day were impressed enough by the teacher's words to really take them seriously in the years that followed. One little boy, however, was impressed. He never forgot the teacher's prediction that "a few will hit upon something that will bring BLESSINGS to the whole world".

The little boy grew up and became a Doctor. But in spite of all the good he did in "mending the broken bodies" that came to him for help, he was not entirely happy nor satisfied. He had not yet found the SECRET.

Then one fine day the "Father of All Blessings" -- whom we call God -- revealed the Cosmic Balance Secret to the Doctor in our story. In case you haven't already guessed, that Doctor is the very one I refer to as "Dr. C" in a previous book: Venusian Health Magic.

No amount of money or material wealth could ever repay "Dr. C" for the health, happiness and joy that his COSMIC BALANCE SECRET has already brought about, and......will continue to bring about in the world.

We can, however, give him full credit for the discovery of the Secret, which is blessing us right now. When I first learned the Secret from "Dr. C", I learned at the same time that he wanted me to teach it to others so that all humanity might be blessed also.

I have taught the Cosmic Balance Secret to you because I wanted to share this blessing with you, that you may be fully equipped with the positive means of coming safely through the Great Turmoil of the World.

After the lecture, a young man -- a student in the local College -- came up to me with a question.

"I was interested," he said, "in your story of how you assisted the little dog by raising his Life-Switch at a distance. It seems to me that if you could do that for animals you could also do it for humans, and so help them, right?"

"Right," I admitted, "It is possible for any awakened individual to do for himself or others the same thing that was done for the dog...IF one knows how to do it and is motivated by a Cosmic Love."

"You may balance me," the young man said, "but only on one condition. That is, that I will not lose anything in the process. That I will retain my individuality! I cannot afford to lose that!"

I at once reassured the student that he would lose nothing by being balanced, that his personality and individuality would express itself better in a balanced body. Upon learning this he was pleased.

I then showed him how he could determine whether his body was balanced or out of balance. Upon checking, he found himself shorter on his right side. The right arm, when compared with the left, was more than one inch shorter in length.

Rather than have him rely or depend upon me or anyone else to "balance" him, I taught him how to balance himself...and within seconds he had grasped the technique -- the Cosmic Balance Secret -- and put it to work bringing himself into perfect balance.

The "Mental Technique" which Violet and I used to assist the little dog, is one of the advanced lessons in re-balancing others. It should not be tried until you have first mastered the Self-Balancing practice. This comes first and is basic. It is of little use to attempt something on a mental level until one is able to perform a physical exercise well enough to bring about perfect balance within himself.

By the way, both techniques -- mental and physical -- accomplish the very same result, which is the expanding of the temporal bones in the cranium...so that the Pituitary Gland (the Life-Switch) has more space in which to "uncramp" itself and restore normal physical balance in the body.

Here is a variation of the Cosmic Balance Secret which you should know about:

Step 1. Sit or stand in relaxed position, with face looking straight in front of you.

Step 2. Place your hands together (like two plates) in front of chest, fingers pointing forward.

Step 3. Now press your hands together as tightly as you can, resisting one hand against the other firmly.

Step 4. While pressing both hands tightly together, lift your eyes upward as high as you can. (Eyes only, not the head.) Hold this position for 5 seconds, then lower eyes and relax yourself. Do not hold the breath.

If you did this correctly, you noticed a feeling of expansion in the area of the forehead above the eyes. That gentle expansion releases the "kinks" and tension in the Life-Switch and gives it more space.

Simple as this Balance Technique may appear, it should not be under-estimated as to its virtues and beneficial effects which are exceedingly marvelous. The method you are now learning required many thousands of hours -- years in fact -- to refine and simplify so that any human being could use it easily.

When you keep yourself "in balance" continually, hour by hour, day by day all through the years, you'll experience for yourself the "proof of the pudding". I have listed some of the observable effects you may expect to realize in your life when you put the Cosmic Balance Secret to work for you every day. We, of course, understand that other factors must not be neglected, if we truly want to be good examples of a NEW ERA.

First of all comes (1) Balance, then (2) Physical purification, (3) Vital Food, (4) Moderate Exercise, (5) Fresh Air, (6) Sunshine, (7) A tranquil mind.

How would you like to improve your "good looks" and hold back the hands of Old Father Time, to the extent that your family and friends are constantly amazed by your youthfulness and natural pep? I'm sure that you, being intelligent, are as interested in that desirable condition as I am. Well, let me assure you that the COSMIC BALANCE SECRET is the one biggest step in "turning back the clock".

Let's take a look at the following list:

GOOD EFFECTS OF BALANCE	BAD EFFECTS OF UN-BALANCE
1. A Straight Body	1. A Crooked body
2. Ease and well-being	2. Dis-Ease & Discomfort
3. Expanded cranium	3. Cramped Cranium
4. A Clear mind	4. A Muddled mind
5. Positive thinking	5. Negative thinking
6. Positive emotions	6. Negative emotions
7. Beauty	7. Ugliness
8. Dynamic Power	8. Weakness
9. Retarded Aging	9. Rapid Aging
10. Self-Confidence	10. Timidity

Given a free choice, which conditions would you choose for yourself and your loved ones? Ah! -- you say you prefer the good effects of balance? That is splendid and of course you know you must stand by your choice and that means you must use the COSMIC BALANCE SECRET <u>daily</u>.

Recently I stopped in to visit with a machinist friend of mine and was deeply impressed by something he told me. He pointed out to me that all good machinists take extra special pains to make sure that the precision machines they intend to use are "on the level" when installed in the shop. If the machines are not setting perfectly level on the floor they soon begin to "vibrate" so much that they are quickly worn out.

The faster the machine runs, the faster it wears itself out -- if it is not level or "balanced". This idea also applies to human beings. We know that the universal law of Equilibrium (Balance) is vitally important to all of us NEW AGE people now, because of two things: (1) The stepped-up cosmic vibration that began in 1960 and will gradually increase, and (2) The Great Turmoil of clashing mental cross-currents in all parts of the world today. We cannot afford to let these "mass-minded" vibrations throw us "off-center"!

RELEASE YOUR COSMIC POWER

Part 5

"Each One Reach One" -- NOW

So vital is the COSMIC BALANCE SECRET to the progress and harmony of the whole world, it cannot be kept a secret any longer. This is where you enter the picture in a most IMPORTANT way. How? Like this:

As soon as you master the technique of "self-balancing" pass the secret on freely to one other person within seven days from the day you yourself learned how to do it.

This simple "chain-reaction" plan of spreading highly important NEW AGE knowledge has already been started by myself and others in dozens of NEW AGE groups all over the country. Nobody on earth can stop it now. It is sweeping like wildfire from one "awakened" individual to another and cannot possibly be halted until all those who are intended by the Creator to know the SECRET have been told about it. No "Anti-Christ" force can stop it.

EACH ONE REACH ONE -- NOW! That is my objective and yours. I am acting under "higher orders" to pass the SECRET along to you, WHY? Because this knowledge is needed by all awakened mankind -- now -- in order that we may set the world stage for A GLORIOUS LIFE in which is no disease or death, in the millenium that is just ahead. Will you march with us my friend, towards the magnificent GOLDEN SUNRISE we are all heading for?

"Is it permissible for me to teach more than one?" you are wondering. The answer: YES! The more you feel impelled to instruct regarding the COSMIC BALANCE SECRET the sooner we will all be enjoying a healthier, happier and nobler LIFE here on this planet.

BUT -- please use your best judgment! I do not want you to rush out and tell the secret to someone who is not open-minded to NEW AGE ideas. You want to reach some sincere soul who will listen to you, not LAUGH at you. No matter what you are attempting to do, if you "cast your pearls--" you know the rest of that story. You must not run the risk of having people SOUR you on the whole idea by laughing at it.

This SECRET is, after all, a sacred thing. We who have been given this priceless information about the "Life-Switch" and the Balance Law are convinced that the whole tremendous question of WHY YOU LIVE and WHY YOU DIE is wrapped up in it. It is, at the very least, the best answer that exists right now.

So use your very best judgment in deciding whom you will reveal the Secret to. Sometimes a complete stranger is more sympathetic and appreciative of our ideas than are members of our own family. However, I am leaving it up to you and your "intuition" to choose the ones you will tell.

Here then, is what you are to do:

1. LEARN the Cosmic Balance Secret yourself. Be able to demonstrate it easily and smoothly, at any time you may be required to do so. Practice the secret immediately upon arising each morning. It is a good idea also to practice it once every afternoon.

2. TEACH the Cosmic Balance Secret to another person within SEVEN days (7 days) after learning it yourself. In teaching others, simply go through the actual motions yourself and have the friend or student imitate what you are doing. It is not necessary for you to touch the other person in order to instruct him successfully in the use of the SECRET. It is legally wise, in fact, to make a special effort NOT to touch your student when teaching this technique.

I once read a statement made by The famous artist Bob Ripley of "Believe It Or Not" fame. Suppose you tell some person a "Secret" and ask him to tell another person that same secret right away. On that basis of each one telling the secret to another one, and assuming there is no break in the chain....your "secret" would travel all around the world in seven days! That -- according to Ripley -- is a FACT, "believe it or not!" Well, Bob, we DO BELIEVE IT!

That's why we've got this COSMIC BALANCE SECRET started on its way around the world by the "person-to-person" chain-reaction system! And -- to prevent a failure somewhere along the line -- we've started a great number of "chains", thousands of them..so that even if there is a "break" in one or more chains, we know that at least ONE will NOT BREAK. It will carry this supremely vital NEW AGE knowledge to all people.

YOU, my friend, are the head of one of these all-important person-to-person chains. Perhaps the chain you start will be the one that spreads out through all the world, helping countless numbers of human beings. I hope it is. And here is a helpful suggestion:

3. EXTRACT a promise from the one who learns the Secret from you, that he or she will in turn pass it on to one (or more) others within seven (7) days. Once you secure a heart-felt promise from another, it is a pretty good sign that he will do what he says.

Why the SEVEN DAY limit? That is to motivate individuals into positive and definite ACTION. We can write and talk all we like about the "Secret", but unless we go into real action and actually demonstrate to others HOW TO DO IT,.........???

EACH ONE REACH ONE -- NOW. This is your test, as it is mine. If we, because of insincerity or lack of courageous daring for the "Cause"-- FAIL in this little test -- the door to our own greater good and the happiness of all mankind -- may close, not to be reopened by some of us during this crucial Time.

Neither words nor excuses can really make up for things we fail to do while we are here. It is like the case of the absent-minded carpenter who showed up on the job without his hammer and as a result the house did not go up that day.

On the other hand, by going into action at once for the Cause of World Balance and Well-Being, you will be assisting the Forces of Light in a wonderful way. Certain "Karmic Debts" you might now have hanging over you will be "written off" as paid in full. This is the time for clearing the Karmic records, and though there are other deeds we shall perform before we reach the GOLDEN SUNRISE, this action is BASIC.

RELEASE YOUR COSMIC POWER

Part 6

"Your Cosmic Power Program"

In this chapter of our book I am going to give you a Program for increasing your supply of Cosmic Power, so that your power for GOOD will steadily increase.

I have found from long experience, that a definite and practical Program is an absolute MUST for individuals who really want to make rapid, positive progress on THE PATH.

Your Cosmic Power Program is very important to you, because it organizes your body, mind and soul for a specific purpose. It points out to you what your purpose really is, then outlines the steps that ought to be followed in order for you to accomplish that purpose...in a positive way. This, then, is a Program designed for a Purpose.

Your Purpose -- and it's an Eternal Purpose -- is to think, feel and act for the highest good of the Cosmic Universe and all of the living beings within it.

That is your "Cosmic Viewpoint", the attitude you need to have and hold if you desire to live into the Golden Age of Peace, Power and Plenty on this earth. Cosmic Power -- and I shall define this term in a simple way very shortly -- will flow into you and through you to bless the whole Universe only when you SEE the Eternal Purpose in your life.

Your greatest strength lies in your purpose. If you see and know your purpose, your objective, you are going to succeed in realizing your spiritual destiny. Seeing your purpose gives you a powerful incentive to move in the desired direction. When you do that, you will see positive results and that will release your enthusiasm...and you will continue making progress.
No purpose equals no action. No action equals failure.

Now let's define "Cosmic Power". If we are going to "release our Cosmic Power" we have to know clearly what we mean by that term, and then we have to know how best to accumulate the Power and send it forth.

Cosmic Power is the universal energy, or solar force which fills all space in the Cosmos. It is the living light of the Logos -- God -- which is sent out into our Cosmic Universe from the "Sun behind the Sun". Because this power comes from a Sun infinitely bigger in size than our own physical Sun, it is also termed the "Super Solar Force" and "The Universal Fire".

Super Solar Force (Cosmic Power) may be described as living, conscious electricity -- of incredible voltage -- and hardly comparable to the form of electricity known to the human race.

This Force can be governed by man, and when governed is the immortal energy which the soul uses to build up man's "Solar" or Spiritual Body. It is this Cosmic Power which every spiritual Initiate must use to strengthen and perfect the "Golden Wedding Garment".

STORING UP SOLAR POWER

If you will agree that all life upon this planet is directly dependent upon the energies sent to it by the Sun of our Solar System...and science now admits that our physical bodies are nothing less than "concentrated sunshine" built up into forms...then the truth is at once realized. We are Sun-powered beings!

Mystics and students of the "Greater Mysteries" have long known that the Sun is supreme within its own system of planets. But they also knew of a greater, "Sun behind the Sun" -- a massive central sun that is situated at the very hub of this Universe, and which influences and controls all other Suns. It is sometimes referred to as the "Supreme Star".

The energy from our physical Sun is known as Solar Force, while the energy from the great Central Sun is known as "Super Solar Force" since it is of much greater strength and positivity.

A time will come when, as you continue progressing on the UPWARD PATH, Super Solar Force will awaken the higher spiritual centers in your brain, into activity. Then you will experience "COSMIC CONSCIOUSNESS" which is higher illumination by the GOD-Spirit.

I would feel terribly remiss in my duty if I did not, at this point in your study, CAUTION you regarding the physical hazards of attempting to force your spiritual progress by "forcing methods" of any kind. These include: "Sitting in the dark for Development", "Concentrating on the Solar Plexus", "Alternate breathing to arouse the fiery Kundalini energy" (Solar force which lies sleeping at base of man's spine). These "forcing methods" are almost always DISASTROUS!

Rather than "force" -- which is always destructive -- my counsel to you is to use "Love" and "Balance" as your spiritual guide-posts. If you seek first the true Kingdom of Heaven (Harmony, Love, Balance) all these things (which are good for you and the universe) shall be added unto you.

You can, however, and should store up a larger supply of Solar Force within your body cells and within your nervous system as this will in no way hinder your spiritual unfoldment nor endanger you. How may you do this in the most healthful and positive way?

Here are two ways I have found highly effective in storing up solar power within my body. (1) By using an abundance of "Solar Foods" in my daily diet; (2) By a definite practice of consciously in-drawing Solar Light Energy into my body for 15 minutes or more three times each week.

THE BEST "SOLAR" FOOD

Sunflower seeds are Mother Nature's one "best" Solar Food for "stepping up" man's vibrations, and increasing his bodily supply of solar energy. I have obtained wonderful results by including Sunflower seeds in my diet each day. I recommend them to you.

Here is how I have benefited from them. Firstly, my energy level is considerably higher both physically and mentally than before using Sunflower Seeds as food. Secondly, I find that I now have more COSMIC POWER to use for assisting other individuals near or distant. You too will derive "Super-Power" from this Super-Food.

Because the Sunflower turns its head and "follows the Sun" all day long, the Seeds are simply drenched in SOLAR ENERGY at its maximum maturity in a food. I find Sunflower Seeds very delicious as well as highly nutritious. But the reason I am recommending them to you now is mainly for their high SOLAR ENERGY CONTENT.

How much should one eat per day? I personally use not less than 2 ounces of the Seeds daily. I like to sprinkle them -- in coarse meal form -- on top of a dish of fresh apples or peaches and add a little fresh cream and natural honey. Simply delicious!

If chewing the seeds presents a problem to you, just place the seeds dry in any good electric blendor (we use the Osterizer) place lid on, then turn on motor to low speed for about half a minute. This will make a wonderful flaky meal of your two ounces of hulled sunflower seed, ready to eat. Never cook solar foods.

Health Food stores are your best source of supply for Sunflower Seeds. Ask for "Hulled Sunflower Seeds" but be sure you do not get chemically treated seeds. I use EL MOLINO brand hulled Sunflower Seeds, packaged by EL MOLINO MILLS, Alhambra, California.

It is best to buy the hulled seeds rather than the packaged Sunflower Seed MEAL. The ground-up Meal may have been on the shelf long enough to turn rancid or slightly bitter. If you grind your own Seeds you are always sure of having sweet-tasting delicious fresh Sunflower Meal that is wholesome and flavorful. Grind only as much as you plan to use in one day. Or, you may prefer not to grind them, but to chew them whole.

HOW TO SET UP YOUR PROGRAM

1. SYSTEM. Every athlete soon discovers that he must be systematic in his physical exercising or the results are almost nil. The same thing is true in the spiritual department of life. Spiritual "muscles" have to be exercised regularly on a systematic basis.

Bodybuilders usually "work out" at least three days every week, on alternate days like Monday, Wednesday and Friday...or Tuesday, Thursday, Saturday. The weekend is left "free" for relaxation and diversion so that the desire to exercise is not diminished.

My suggestion to you is to follow a similar plan for building up positive SPIRITUAL POWER. You are going to find that this will be far more IMPORTANT and VITAL to you than physical body power from now on.

You must not, however, allow yourself to use this as an excuse to neglect your physical body. Remember, body and mind rise and fall together" and your mentality must be kept keen, quick and alert. Here is one effective way to SCHEDULE your Personal Power Program:

DAY OF WEEK   ACTIVITY

1. Monday............Physical
2. Tuesday...........Spiritual
3. Wednesday.........Physical
4. Thursday..........Spiritual
5. Friday............Physical
6. Saturday.........---------
7. Sunday............Spiritual

On this suggested schedule, you devote special attention to the care, feeding and exercise of your physical body on three alternate days that are most suitable to you. Follow whatever mode of exercising appeals to you: hiking, climbing, swimming, calisthenics, weight-lifting, eurythmic dancing, tennis, etc.

In physical exercising always strive to better your previous attempts. Don't be satisfied to remain on the same physical level forever, but keep doing a little better each time and improve yourself.

Spiritual development follows the same law of improvement and "progression". By setting three definite days in every week for spiritual exercises and NEW AGE practices, you will build power quickly.

You may now begin to think of yourself as a "Spiritual Athlete" in training for greater work with the GOLDEN LEGION of awakened souls everywhere. I shall give you four (4) special practices to follow, in the next chapter of this book. Before you do the practices I want you to write down your SCHEDULE now, of the 3 days you will devote each week for realizing and increasing your COSMIC POWER. Write your SCHEDULE on an easy-to-read sheet of paper or on a card and post it on your home bulletin board, or where you will see it.

RELEASE YOUR COSMIC POWER

Part 7

"Releasing The Cosmic Power"

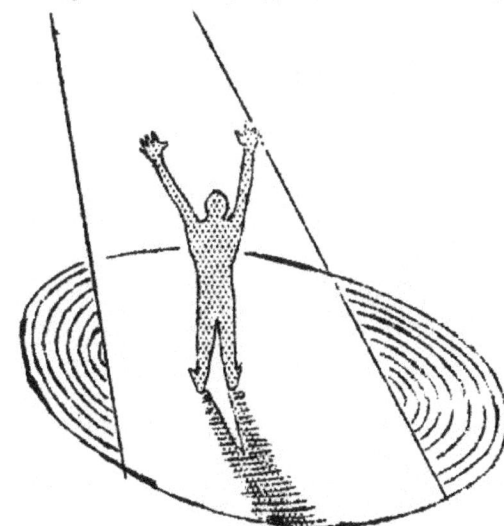

THE COSMIC POWER that runs the universe, spins the planets in their orbits, and which fills all space -- is the same Cosmic Power that gives you LIFE. If your contact with that "living, conscious electricity" is positive, you will express MORE ABUNDANT LIFE. In this chapter I shall reveal FOUR (4) special practices you may use at once to "recharge" yourself with Cosmic Power or universal energy.

I shall also explain how you may best RELEASE your increased power in a way that will bring about endless new JOY and HAPPINESS..not only to you but to the Universe.

THE BIG KEY, the basic secret of attracting Cosmic Power to you is to work on a principle known to all mystics as "the law of Correspondences". More simply, that means "Like Attracts Like" in the mental and spiritual realms.

We make use of that basic principle by realizing in our mind that we are far more than mere physical human bodies. We are SUNS. Just as the Solar Sun in the sky "out-shines" life, love and light to all its planets, so do we "outshine" our life, love and light into our world -- and even beyond.

THIS IS THE SECRET. You must begin now to think of yourself as a "Sun" that must out-shine and not repress any of the natural activity of life, love and intelligence. The more you realize how much of a "Sun" you really are, the greater will be your affinity for LIFE, LOVE and LIGHT from the great "Sun behind the Sun".

To prepare yourself for the practices that follow, check yourself at this time to make sure you are in good BALANCE and HARMONY before you proceed.

Sit or stand in a comfortable, relaxed posture, with body straight and back of head in line with your spine. Let your breathing rate be somewhat slower than usual. This helps to reduce excessive speed of the mental action and keeps you calm and poised. Time duration of each Practice may vary according to needs. Repeat the following affirmation silently, 3 times:

    I AM A TRUE SPIRITUAL SUN!
    I OUT-SHINE LIFE, LOVE, LIGHT!

This strengthens your mental and spiritual affinity with the Cosmic Power of the universe. Now you are ready for special practice Number 1.

IN-DRAWING THE COSMIC ENERGY

(Practice No. 1)

(1) Quiet the mind by breathing slowly 3 times.

(2) Tune-out all negative thoughts by telling brain and body to "Be still and know I AM, I AM I, I AM THAT I AM."

(3) Raise your arms, extending them toward the Sun or the heavens. Spread your fingers fanwise, close your eyes and feel the vibrations of LIFE FORCE beginning to flow into and through your body.

(4) Say silently (or audibly if with a group):

    I AM LIFE! (3 times)
    I AM LOVE! "   "
    I AM LIGHT! "   "

(5) Now bring both hands together above your head, closing fingers together so that hands are in praying position above you. Then keeping hands locked together, lower your arms to your chest exactly in front of the heart. Point fingers straight ahead.

(6) Keeping your thumbs and fingertips together, turn your fingers so they point to your heart. This is very beneficial, and strengthens the Cosmic Light Circuit between heart and head. EXHALE for 7 counts. As you exhale, direct the Cosmic Life Force to enter the heart, recharging it and the brain centers. The

secret of this and all the other special practices is to do them in a conscious manner. Know in your own mind what you want to accomplish and then do it with your thinking, willing and feeling, in concentration.

* * * * *

PROJECTING THE ENERGY TO OTHERS

(Practice No. 2)

(1) Take in Cosmic Energy as in Practice No. 1.

(2) Speak to the Father Within, your Higher Self and say: "Thy Will, not mine, be done!" This eliminates the little self will...puts you in tune with the Cosmic Will and lets in POWER, LOVE, WISDOM.

(3) Extend both arms straight in front of you and slowly fill your lungs with air, taking a breath of air to each count while counting to 7.

(4) Point your arms in direction of the person to whom you wish to send the Power. If you do not know the exact direction, spread your fingers fanwise.

(5) Exhale slowly while counting to 7, and as you are exhaling, WILL the Cosmic Energy to instantly travel to the person whom you are visualizing.

(6) Re-charge yourself and relax.

* * * * *

RELEASING THE COSMIC BALANCE LIGHT

(Practice No. 3)

THE Cosmic Green Light is the BALANCING ray, and exerts an exceedingly potent effect whenever it is used. It stabilizes, balances, quiets and relaxes. In the color spectrum, green is mid-way between the highest and the lowest color energies. You will find abundant use for the Cosmic Green energy as conditions grow more turbulent, chaotic and violent in the world from now on. Each member of the GOLDEN LEGION on Earth is expected to release the clear Cosmic Green Light in full strength during all times of crisis and discord. So let us read on and learn how to do this effectively.

The Practice is as follows:

(1) Close your eyes, relax and visualize a large white sun sitting in the sky above you. Keep watching that sun mentally until it appears very white. When it does, look at the exact center of that Sun.

(2) Now bring to mind the memory of the color GREEN as it appears in most traffic signal lights..a brilliant clear green. Mentally see a narrow beam or ray of that COSMIC GREEN LIGHT emanating out of the center of the Sun, and entering your forehead.

(3) While you are imaging the charging color mentally, you must begin the Master Breath: Inhale slowly to count of 7 and hold for 1 count.

(4) Now you have breathed in the COSMIC GREEN LIGHT on your inhaling breath. You have charged your own centers of balance and brought yourself into harmony. Next step is to send out the charge to others.

(5) Hold a mental image in mind of the one you desire to assist, and slowly EXHALE to count of 7. At each count you must think, feel and will the force of the COSMIC GREEN LIGHT to project out from you instantly and charge the one you are thinking of. SEE the light raying out in a beam from your forehead and entering middle of other person's forehead. This must all be done with a transcendent feeling of high Love.

* * * *

DIAMOND STAR MEDITATION

(Practice No. 4)

Your closing practice is a powerful meditative invocation. When you are entirely alone and undisturbed and in a very peaceful state of mind..gaze for 60 full seconds at the illustration of THE DIAMOND on page 32.

When the image of the diamond is strong, clear, and vivid in your mind, close your eyes. Now see the diamond mentally as being directly in front of you... and EXPANDING IN SIZE rapidly until it is large enough for you to step inside of that diamond. As soon as it is that size you must mentally step inside and begin to perform the Master Breath (Inhale 7 counts -- Hold for 1 count -- Exhale for 7 counts -- Hold for 1 count.)

On the inhaling breath, which is done very slowly, <u>will</u> that your vibration be raised with each count. Make a mental request of your High Self (Spiritual Guardian) to protect you by keeping your vibrational "uplift" within safe limits for you at this time.

Affirm: "I AM LIGHT!" with each count while inhaling.

When count of 7 is reached, hold for one count and realize mentally and emotionally whatever change you are experiencing in your personal vibrations. Notice also how tremendously BRIGHT AND SCINTILLATING the Diamond sphere, in which you are standing (mentally) has now become. This realization increases with each practice.

Begin now to exhale slowly to count of 7, and at each count send out your increased LIGHT, LOVE AND LIFE into the UNIVERSAL Ethers to bless all living beings. After finishing the count of 7, hold breath for count of 1 and relax. Conclude by directing mentally that the Diamond recede in size to its original size.

Open your eyes now and look again at the Diamond illustrated on page 32. Meditate for a while on the spiritual truth that a CENTRAL LIGHT or DIAMOND STAR dwells within you and within all mankind. It is your "Divine Spark" or Spiritual Light. This Light is the Star of the True or Divine Will of the Universe. It is of the most intense brilliance, like a great Diamond. You and I and all men may freely place our own little personal wills in line with its Guidance.

There is a wondrous MYSTERY and glorious purpose to the above Practice of the DIAMOND STAR MEDITATION. I must not reveal this to you now, but to all those who faithfully do this Practice regularly, will come the full and complete revelation <u>from within</u>.

Will you, my Friend, unfold the sacred mystery of the DIAMOND STAR? I believe that you will, because I have deep faith and belief in you...as one of the Golden Legion.

You can use these Cosmic Power Practices to aid other human beings, to bring healing LIFE to others.

THE SHAVER MYSTERY AND THE INNER EARTH

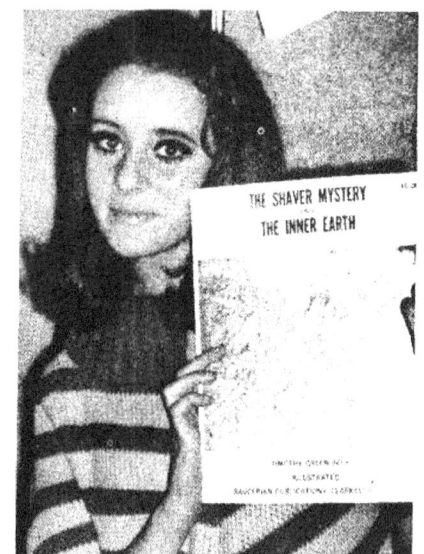

At long last the TRUTH about the most astounding mystery of our time can be told without unneeded psychic trimmings and destorted editing. Direct from the pen of Timothy Green Beckley comes the book that is officially approved by Richard Shaver himself.

In this volume you will learn the amazing truth as to the actual origin for the Flying Saucers and why they are coming to Earth.

You'll read some of the most hair-raising and chilling accounts ever put down on paper. Such as the disappearance of Steve Brodie and his capture by the Dero. Of attacks on surface people by various creatures whose existence cannot now be denied.

Chapters and comments by such researchers as:

Dr. T. Lobsang Rampa - Dand Howard - Rev. Frank Stranges

See actual maps showing the EXACT location of the mystical city of ice "Rainbow City" - Rare hand paintings of the Jersey Devil - Never before published photographs of Pre-Deluge Artifacts.

Introduction by the author of THEY KNEW TOO MUCH ABOUT FLYING SAUCERS - Gray Barker.

Appendix by Ray Palmer former editor of AMAZING STORIES who first published Shaver's astounding accounts.

THE SHAVER MYSTERY AND THE INNER EARTH is a large 8-1/2 x 11 volume of 125 pages, the largest of this format we have published. Copies now $5.00.

 **ALSO READ THESE STARTLING NEW BOOKS ON UFOS**

1. MY VISIT TO VENUS by Dr. T. Lobsang Rampa. Did the famed Tibetan Lama actually visit Venus, or did he travel there astrally? $2.00

2. FLYING SAUCERS ARE WATCHING YOU by John Sherwood. The book that puts you inside the great Michigan flap. Photos, illustrations, etc. $3.95

3. UFO WARNING by John Stuart. Beset by strange occult forces and terrible warnings the author encounters a lecherous monster. . . . $3.95

4. WE MET THE SPACE PEOPLE by the Mitchell Sisters. Two young sisters discuss their contacts with aliens from Mars and Venus. . . . $1.10

5. STRANGE CASE OF DR. M.K. JESSUP edited by Gray Barker. New evidence that Dr. Jessup was silenced by the "men in black". $3.95

6. THE RETURN OF GEORGE ADAMSKI by E. Buckle. 2 days after his death the controversial contactee is said to have made contact with an English gardner. Learn of poltergeist like beings kidnapping people from Earth. Strange phone calls and tape recordings containing alien voices, etc. $5.95

7. DOCUMENT 96 by Frank Martin Chase. Lavishly illustrated volume suggests some saucers may be built by terrestrials - maybe the Nazis! $5.00

8. FLYING SAUCERS IN THE BIBLE by Virginia Brasington. The Bible contains many accounts of visitations of space people. Beautifully and inspiringly written $3.95

9. THE BOOK OF SPACE SHIPS AND THEIR RELATIONSHIPS WITH THE EARTH, by the God of a Planet Near the Earth and Others. Space communications of particularly inspiring nature. $3.95

Order From
SAUCERIAN BOOKS
Box 2228
Clarksburg, W. Va. 26301
WRITE FOR COMPLETE BOOK LIST

```
Dear Sir:
    Please send me Shaver Mystery & inner Earth at $5.00.
    Send me following books listed by number_____
    Name_____
    Address_____ City_____ State_____ Zip_____
```

Flying Saucer Revelations

by

Michael X

FLYING SAUCER REVELATIONS

- by -

MICHAEL X

* * *

This is an Educational and Inspirational Course of Study dealing with Interplanetary subjects. It is especially written and intended for NEW AGE Individuals everywhere. The following FIVE lessons are included in this special Study:

1. "THE SAUCER PEOPLE ON EARTH"

2. "FLYING SAUCERS AT GIANT ROCK"

3. "SECRETS OF THE SAUCER PEOPLE"

4. "THE MAGIC OF ETHER SHIPS"

5. "DISCS, DESTINY AND YOU"

* * * * *

"FLYING SAUCER REVELATIONS" is based on Scientific Findings, UFO data accumulated by numerous Researchers, intensive Personal Investigation and Mystical Revelation by the Author.

The Saucer People On Earth

by

MICHAEL X

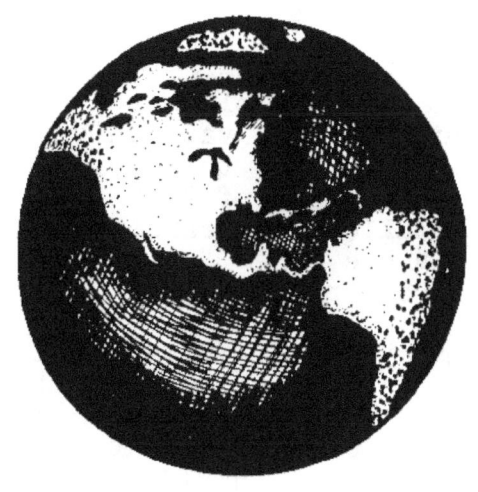

Mystic Monograph No. 1

MYSTIC MONOGRAPH   NUMBER ONE

"SAUCER PEOPLE ON EARTH"

Part One

Man's Secret Origin

Did you ever wonder about how you came to be on this planet? Where did you...and the other billions of human inhabitants of this Earth come from in the first place? What are the real facts?

You're going to be astounded and amazed when you find out the whole story of man's secret origin! You'll probably say to yourself "Why wasn't this information brought to my attention before?" and, "Why wasn't I taught this kind of knowledge in school, so I could have been making good use of it all these years? Why? Why? Why?

Well, for one thing, this is MYSTIC KNOWLEDGE. You can't expect to learn it in school, unless of course, it's a Mystic School. How many Mystic Schools are there? You can count them on the fingers on one hand. This is SECRET KNOWLEDGE. It's not commonly known at all. In fact, it is so rare and uncommon that as a general rule you have to search diligently for it, and "prove yourself" before it is revealed to you. That is why I'm going to give you certain facts-- some golden links in the chain of your GOOD--which have been so long withheld from you. I believe you are now ready for the great TRUTHS!

WHERE DID MAN COME FROM ? ?   The fact is, Earthman is not the only tenant of this universe. He only thinks he is. That is where he makes a big mistake. There are countless other Solar Systems throughout this vast universe in which highly intelligent human life forms are, at this very moment, living and breathing the same as you and I! Many of those Systems are not merely hundreds or thousands, but MILLIONS of years in advance of ours...and the beings who inhabit those other "planetary chains" have a great deal to do with YOUR secret origin.

According to many of the ancient teachings, ALL of the planets of this Solar System are inhabited by intelligent beings. Now I did not say PHYSICAL HUMAN BEINGS, such as are on Earth. It's mightily important for you to realize that some of the planets in our System are peopled only by ETHERIC BEINGS. They don't have physical bodies like we do. But they do have a very efficient etheric body which they are very proud of, and which serves them nicely in many ways.

All beings--whether in physical or etheric form--are of course in varying grades of intelligence or "awareness of that which is". Each planet, for example, in our System is said to be actually a "School of Life" wherein the intelligent beings are able to learn certain vitally essential lessons in the true art of living.

Just as in any school, the idea is for all the individuals who dwell on any planet, to master the various "rules" or "laws" of life.

This is accomplished, of course, by learning how to consciously expand our awareness of the secret principles upon which your mind and your body and the entire universe are run.

When this is accomplished--and ONLY then--to the extent that an individual actually applies the knowledge he gains, he or she is permitted to "graduate" to another planet more advanced in the planetary scheme, where NEW LESSONS are learned. In this way, we progress from glory to glory...constantly unfolding our higher God-like powers!

Since there are a total of nine planets revolving around the Sun, it seems we Earthlings have Nine Schools to attend before we complete our "Course of Study" in this Solar System.

Each "School Term" lasts 2500 years. (Figuring in Cosmic Time this is not as long as you might think). At the end of that planetary cycle, some evolutionary cataclysm usually occurs (such as the Glacial Age, the Deluge, a Polar Shift, etc.) which, quite naturally, eliminates the "mass-minded" or the ones who "failed" in the earthly School of Life.

At the crucial time, however, some great Teacher of Light and Love appears on the planet. His purpose is to guide and direct the next class of intelligent beings who are arriving on the earthly scene for the first time. Jesus, Buddha, Zoroaster, Lao-Tse, Hermes Trismegistus, and Sanat Kumara (The Ancient of Days) were among the greatest of these Teachers. You could name many others.

What I am about to give you now is not new information. Rather, it is ages old. In fact, it is part of a body of Secret Knowledge that is called the Ageless Wisdom, for it is eternal. Some of this information is older than our planet itself (meaning it was given to us by higher intelligences from other planets and other systems.) Fortunately for you and me and other sincere Seekers, this marvelous body of knowledge has been preserved by a rare few of Earth's mystic masters in India, Tibet, Europe and America. The "Saucer Story" for instance, is an amazingly ancient story...known to certain advanced Earthlings for many, many centuries.

Before revealing the full story, I shall first "condition" your mind to several facts regarding interplanetary or space flight. The first thing to realize is that SPACE FLIGHT IS POSSIBLE. Our men of science on Earth now admit it. They believe that within the next ten years we shall have launched a rocket-ship to the moon and back. (They are even now experimenting in the building of our own "discs".)

This being so, what, I ask you, is there to have prevented some other planet, more highly advanced than our Earth, from having reached the same conclusion long ago. And, having reached such a definite conclusion, what is there to have stopped them from building a Space Ship in the logical form of a Flying Disc, and, using a better power than rocket power, conquering Space?!

Let us carry this thought a little further. Why do you think it is so difficult, so contrary to the thinking habits of our modern scientists to accept the idea that Flying Saucers already exist?

I will tell you why. If our "learned" scientists were to admit the existence of Spacecraft and Beings from other worlds, they would be admitting that our planet Earth is NOT the one and only planet in the Universe which has produced highly intelligent life forms. To admit such a thing would be a terrible blow to man's proud ego. It would force man to accept the fact that Earth is not the advanced place some of us think it is. Earth Man doesn't like to admit this.

The truth, according to ancient Hindu writings, is that Earth is but a "baby" in comparison to other planets in the universe. For example, Venus is one entire Chain (period of evolution) in advance of ours. Therefore, the intelligences of Venus are very highly evolved. This had to be, for the Venusian Race is ancient beyond belief in the sense that it originated many millions of years ago.

As for the story of the first consciously awakened Man on Earth, it really begins in the year 18,617,841 B.C. In other words, the date of our epic is eighteen million, six hundred and seventeen thousand, eight hundred and forty-one years before the birth of Christ.

In that momentous year--as revealed by ancient Hindu writings-- the first space ship came from the planet Venus, to land here on planet Earth. From Venus, "The Home of the Gods", came Sanat Kumara, (The Lord of the Flame) with his four Great Lords and one hundred assistants. These shining beings saw to it that human souls became incarnated in physical bodies on Earth.

Until the arrival on Earth of Sanat Kumara from Venus, Man did not have conscious awareness. He was the product of long ages of slow evolving upon planet Earth. Physically he resembled Man as we know him today; but mentally he was like the animals. That is, he lived only in his subconsciousness. The front section of his brain was asleep.

When the Lord of the Flame saw the poor mindless thing that was Man, he felt moved to assist directly in Man's unfoldment. He used his spiritual powers to awaken the centers of individuality in the Earth Man.

This fact is the "missing link" in the evolution of Man on this planet.

The Lord Sanat Kumara called the first consciously awakened man Adam, in tribute to the Venusian Lords who belonged to the Adamic Race of Venus. At the time of his conscious awakening, Adam's body was androgynous or bi-sexual. He was a two-fold being, having both male and female components perfectly balanced within his own physical body. To facilitate the propagation of offspring, Sanat Kumara changed the sex polarity of Adam from bi-sexual to uni-sexual. This led to the creation of Eve who became Adam's mate.

Adam and Eve were blessed with children and the Adamic line

branched out to cover the entire face of the globe. All of us here on Earth--regardless of color, or of "belief-conditioning"--are direct descendants of Adam and Eve; and indirect descendants of the Adamic Race of Venus.

After Sanat Kumara and his helpers had finished their work of starting a physical race of Mankind on Earth, they returned again to Venus and left man to evolve higher up the ladder of Life through his own personal efforts and illuminating experiences. It was only right that the Lord Thinkers should leave Man then, for those brilliant Beings belonged to an entirely different Life Chain than ours.

As the centuries of time rolled by, men of Earth learned many secrets of universal power, secrets which most people of today believe to be strictly modern and "new" discoveries of science. The hidden truth however, is that what we call new is "old stuff" to the Saucer People of the inhabited planets in space. They've been masters of a "Secret Science" of the universe which is so ancient its origin is lost in the mists of time. Some of their truths are not millions, but billions and trillions of years old. Much of the knowledge has been passed from one planet to another, such as the "formula" for successful Space Flight, De-Gravitation, Telethot, etc. etc. There simply is nothing essentially NEW under the sun; though our modern science likes to think so.

As Man's "I.Q." increased, wonderful civilizations such as those on Atlantis, Lemuria and Mu, were built..but each time they fell apart or were destroyed chiefly through misuse of their own great powers. In addition to the calamitous results of human foolishness, Nature itself rebelled many times. Great planetary cataclysms occurred, due to a sudden shifting of the poles of the Earth. The Great Deluge, or Flood, was one of these. It is important, because it is part of the whole amazing story of Flying Saucers, the Space People, who they are and what their seemingly "mysterious" purpose really is.

Way back in the days of Noah, the Earth shifted its poles. At once a monstrous Tidal Wave swept over all of the then populated areas of the world, destroying nearly all living beings. All the marvelous ancient records, manuscripts, secrets, etc., were lost to mankind, and man was forced to begin again his long upward climb toward the Light. Did I say ALL was lost? Not quite all. We must not forget the fabulous "Bible in Stone"--THE GREAT PYRAMID OF EGYPT! Let us now see how the Great Pyramid "ties in" to the picture.

Shortly before the Noaic Deluge took place, the Saucer People had realized that such a disaster was impending. They could tell, from their observations made in space, that the Earth was about to SHIFT POSITION. In the short time remaining before the "shift" was to occur, the Saucer People--Venusians--went into positive action on behalf of humanity's present and future welfare. The Lords of Venus determined to build an "altar to the Lord in the midst of the land of Egypt, and a pillar at the border thereof to the Lord. And it shall be for a SIGN and for a WITNESS unto the Lord of Hosts in the land of Egypt."--Isaiah 19:19-20.

You no doubt are aware that the Great Pyramid was designed by beings of extraordinary intelligence. The perfect knowledge of Astronomy revealed by the Pyramid was "first-hand" knowledge possessed by those Masters of Space and Time, the Lords of Venus!

Inner teaching has it that the Lord Thinkers directed one of Earth's wisest mortals, King Thothmus, as to HOW the entire edifice was to be constructed. Thothmus was a great mystic, and cooperated fully with the Venusians for he understood that the building of the Great Pyramid would serve FIVE vital purposes:

1. To preserve Secret Knowledge on Earth.
2. To prophesy the future of Earthmen.
3. To serve as a Temple of Mystic Truth.
4. To be a SIGN or landmark for Space Ships.
5. To be a WITNESS unto the Lord of Hosts.

As you know, certain principles of construction were used which are still the wonder of the world, even today. For instance, so accurately were the stones interlocked in the Pyramid that you can scarcely insert a calling card between the blocks, today.

The "Lord of Hosts" refers to that highly evolved and mighty being, Jesus Christ, whose kingdom was of "another world" ("not of this world")....a planet in our Solar System that is far ahead of us in spiritual unfoldment. This highly spiritual soul was be be born on Earth, and become an outstanding Teacher of Light and Love.

So the Pyramid was built and the Knowledge of Ages concealed within its stone walls, to endure down through the centuries. Noah, a sincere seeker of spiritual Light, was contacted by the Saucer People and warned of the planetary shifting that was soon to destroy the Men of Planet 3 (Earth). So Noah built an Ark as directed.

THEN THE EARTH SHOOK TERRIBLY!

And the oceans ROARED over the land, flooding ALL of the populated areas. "And the waters prevailed exceedingly upon the Earth; and all the high hills, that were under the whole heaven, were covered. Fifteen cubits upward did the waters prevail; and the MOUNTAINS were covered. And ALL FLESH DIED that moved upon the Earth, both of fowl, and of cattle, and of beast, and of every creeping thing upon the Earth, and EVERY MAN. All in whose nostrils was the breath of life, of ALL that was in the dry land, died."--Genesis 7:19.

NOAH and his few faithful followers were, of course, spared... so that the Race could continue as the Lord Thinkers had planned. And so it has continued to this day.

Only one thing is wrong. Some of us Earthlings, too many of us, in fact, have refused to grow as fast in the spiritual department of life as we have grown in the mental, technical and material phases of living. How very deplorable! We've been told time and time again, "With all thy getting, get understanding!" That means SPIRITUAL WISDOM does it not? What do you think our nation, in fact our whole world NEEDS most right now? More Guided Rocket Missiles? More Super-Sonic Jet Bombers? More A-Bombs and H-Bombs in our "stockpile"?

No. A million times NO! You know the answer as well as I. We need a dynamic SPIRITUAL AWAKENING! We need to send out a great LOVE-RAY to our fellowman in every country, and lift him up into a higher kind of "response". But in order to send out such a Love-Ray we must ourselves, individually as well as collectively, feel and experience this dynamic SPIRITUAL AWAKENING. We must cease smothering our spiritual wisdom. We must refuse to let it be choked out by the wasted attentions we give to matters which are NOT Spiritual. Only the true LOVE-RAY(which our Greatest of Teachers explained to us 2,000 years ago) can nullify the effect of the horrible DEATH-RAY that man keeps "tinkering" with.

THE AIR FORCE NOW BUILDS OWN FLYING SAUCERS. The Department of Defense in our country just recently released a most interesting report, prepared by the United States Air Force. It stated that a new type of "vertical rising, DISC-shaped aircraft is now being built for the Air Force by AVRO, Ltd., Canada. Why build a Flying Saucer? For several good reasons. It can take off vertically without any need of a large landing field. Once it is in horizontal flight, it will be capable of enormous SPEED.

Soon you'll be seeing plenty of "Saucers" in the sky, produced by Earthmen, if the AVRO project turns out successfuly. We hope it works out for them, for we understand they've poured six million dollars into the project already. Back in 1945 the Air Force did not put much "stock" in the real "existence" of Flying Discs, even when the Discs were buzzing all around Washington, D. C., the seat of our Government.

In the Air Force report, which you can read in the April 1956 issue of Fantasy and Science Fiction magazine (on your newsstands or send 35¢ to Fantasy House, Inc. 471 Park Ave., New York 22, N. Y.)-- the findings of their "Saucer Investigations" during the past three years are--to our way of thinking--still very"inconclusive". The idea of an extra-terrestial origin of the "Unidentified Aerial Objects" is carefully avoided.

Authorities can sometimes be quite misleading. Perhaps for a valid reason, such as "security" measures, or to avert public panic. We can understand this. But let us, you and I, think for ourselves with the evidence before us. The real Truth about the Discs, the landing of the Saucer People on Earth, and their vital mission, will thus be revealed to us by our own "Knower" within!

This "Knower" within is the revealer of all true wisdom and can be contacted by keeping your attention upon the Great True Self, or God-Presence within your own heart. It is only by devotion to this spiritual center within you that the "Knower" reveals true wisdom. The wisest men who ever lived on earth attained wisdom in this way!

* * * * *

A PERSONAL NOTE

The Truth is never impossible; merely incredible. When we expand our personal awareness beyond the norm, all of Life's "mysteries" vanish. They become new truths made plain! Happily, Truth is no respecter of persons. That is why Visitors from Space have made contact with Earthlings from many different walks of life. Let us now consider some of those contacts, and discover what they mean to you, to me, and to all the people of Earth.

                THE AUTHOR

"SAUCER PEOPLE ON EARTH"

Part Two

The Contacts

The average person still is inclined to consider the subject of "Flying Saucers" as a huge joke. Mention the words to your next door neighbor and you will instantly know, from the reaction you get, what I mean.

That is regrettable. Flying Saucers are in no sense a joking matter. Flying Saucers are REALITIES. Interplanetary flight is a REALITY. And the Saucer People are also living REALITIES. I wish I could make these points even more emphatic. The time for joking is past. We must learn the true facts and the real meaning of the Saucers. And we must accept the facts for what they are.

NON-TERRESTIAL ORIGIN OF THE FLYING SAUCERS. Literally millions of people on earth have sighted Spacecraft. In fact, they have been seen by earthlings for countless centuries, and so recorded by astronomers and historians of all races and countries on Earth. All attempts to "debunk" the existence of the Flying Saucers in no way invalidates the authentic facts, carefully gathered from all over the world, which PROVE that Unidentified Flying Objects of amazing character, and of a non-terrestial origin have been, and still are being seen.

Let's go backwards a bit in time to the year 1519. The place, Old Mexico. The Aztec Indians, under the rule of Montezuma, were in their glory. They had conquered most of the country, were rich and powerful. But they practiced HUMAN SACRIFICE to an extent never equalled by any race in the history of the world. This was something directly contrary to all the laws of the Space People (as well as to the law of their own great teacher, Quetzal-Coatl).

In order to end the evil practice and disperse the powerful Aztecs forever, the "Lord Thinkers" sent a series of mysterious and frightening "omens" to the king Montezuma. Omens included a prediction of the exact date on which the white men under Cortes, would conquer the Aztecs. A vision of the future gathered from the land of the dead by Montezuma's sister. And lastly, brilliant lights in the night sky. Let me describe those 'lights" more fully.

On the eastern horizon of Mexico, appeared a tremendously large, brightly glowing object shaped somewhat like a triangle. It was so brilliant that it lighted up the whole countryside and could be seen from midnight till dawn for a period of FORTY DAYS!

Another strange omen was the mysterious "disintegration" of two stone temples (in which human sacrifice was performed) by some powerful ray coming from the Spaceship which hovered overhead. An account of all these happenings can be found in the ancient history books and legends of Old Mexico, showing that Saucers are not NEW.

Now let us move swiftly up to more modern times to the year 1952...to be precise, the night of July 29, 1952. The place, Miami Florida. There had been a flurry of "sightings" of Flying Saucers in the Miami Area during both June and July, so one young U. S. Marine photographer (now out of uniform) was alert and ready with his movie camera to "catch" a Saucer on film. PIC Magazine for June 1954, printed an article by Ralph Mayher, the determined young photographer who proved on film that Flying Saucers are REAL.

Mr. Mayher's movie film lasted a full three minutes. It showed a glowing, disc-like object in motion, which became closer and brighter in each frame of the picture. It moved with an incredible speed. How fast? Ralph Mayher sent his movie film to the University of Florida physics department for a calculated report.

7550 miles per hour...was their figure! That's at least 5550 miles per hour FASTER than any of our high-speed super-sonic jets! In his letter reporting the calculated speed of the object, the assistant Professor of Physics at the University expressed his belief that the "saucer" did not travel at this high speed for the full three minutes. Rather, it came into sight at a much SLOWER speed, then accelerated into tremendous velocity and sped away.

If our own world's fastest Guided Missiles are only capable of travelling at a speed of around 2,000 miles an hour; then isn't it only logical that these "U.F.O's" have an interplanetary origin... and do NOT originate here on this Earth at all?

Time: February, 1956. Place: Alameda County near San Francisco. Sargent Larry White of the Alameda County office saw some spectacular purplish "lights" in the sky, as he glanced up from his patrol car on Stonybrook road near Decoto. The lights were gigantic in size and could be seen for nearly 45 minutes between clouds. They looked like giant "railroad flairs" to Sargent White and others. The San Francisco newspapers carried the story next day.

Saucers are today's biggest "mystery". That is, they are a mystery to those whose minds are tightly closed against the Truth. But the Truth about Flying Saucers has been with us for "lo, these many years." You need only seek and you will be astounded.

The Bible mentions them many times. It refers to them as the "fiery chariots of the Lord". Listen to this sentence from Isaiah 66:15, "For behold, the Lord will come with fire, and with his chariots..." And read Psalm 68:17, "The chariots of God are twenty thousand..." And do not overlook 2nd Kings, 2:11. It says, "Will he return from heaven as he went, by a whirlwind, and in a chariot of fire?" Aren't these "chariots" merely another way of describing the objects that Kenneth Arnold named "Flying Saucers"?

Ezekiel gives this fascinating account of Flying Saucers in Chapter 1:16 of the Bible. "The appearance of the Wheels and their work was like unto the color of a beryl (bluish green stone) and their appearance and their work was as it were a wheel in the middle of a wheel." (NOTE: Read all of Chapt. 1 of Exekiel.)

The fact is, Flying Saucers are continually appearing in greater numbers in different parts of the world (France, Russia, Mexico, England, Australia, as well as the United States). The question is, why? Whence do they come? and what do they want?

The inhabitants of other planets (both the etheric and physical people who live on other worlds) realize that we Earthlings have the atomic bomb and the even worse Hydrogen bomb. They know that all-out atomic warfare on Earth could wipe out the race of Man almost overnight. It could also have dire effects on the entire universe, since all things interact in the great Cosmic Scheme.

Not only might the Earthlings--in their stupidity--succeed in blowing themselves to bits; but they might also affect seriously the etheric regions which surround our planet and its stratosphere. The Etherean Beings certainly have no intention of permitting such an etheric disaster to occur. Not if they can prevent it.

On at least a dozen occasions, the Space People have been known to land their Spacecraft and converse with people of Earth. And... at least eight persons from our Earth have assertedly been aboard their ships and had enlightening talks with the Saucerians. Three persons, Dan Frey, George Van Tassel, and Orfeo Angelucci, assert they have not only been aboard a Space Ship; but have enjoyed an actual RIDE in the amazing craft.

On August 24th of 1953, George Van Tassel of Giant Rock in Yucca Valley, California, was wakened out of his sleep around 2 A.M. The strange visitor who stood before him at the foot of his bed spoke to him, saying: "My name is Solgonda. I would be pleased to show you our craft."

"From the time I got out of bed, until I returned to it," says George, "Every time I thought of something to say he was answering me before I could speak the first word of any sentence. This proved to me their perfect ability to communicate by Thought Transference."

As they approached the Ship, George began to get "butterflies" in his stomach from about fifty feet away. On getting nearer, his hair seemed to want to stand up on end. (NOTE: Magnetic force-fields of great strength can create this effect.)

On entering the Space Ship the feeling immediately disappeared. Solgonda showed George around the Ship, demonstrating the various instruments used for celestial space navigation. Even the "engine" was seen clearly enough so that George could mentally grasp something of the advanced principle by which it operated. After about 20 minutes of sheer elation to say nothing of revelation, George was accompanied by Solgonda back to George's bed and the strange visitation was terminated.

What do these "contacts" tell us" Many things...strange to us and wonderful. Firstly, the beings from space are NOT warlike.

If they were, we'd have been annihilated centuries ago. No, they are here to help...not harm us. In fact, the very laws of the universe by which they live will not permit them to harm us. It is through helping Earth Man to understand life, and his right relation to the Cosmos and his fellow beings, that the "Lord Thinkers" of other worlds advance themselves in the great scheme of things!

Remember the planetary "Schools of Life". They are governed by a simple rule. The closer a planet is to the center of a given Solar System, that is, its Sun, the more intense LIGHT it receives from that Sun. The higher also are its spiritual vibrations. In other words, the inhabitants of such a planet are <u>filled with light</u> hence are more highly intelligent and spiritual.

Conversely, the farther away a planet is from its Sun, the less LIGHT its inhabitants are able to receive. Thus they are proportionately less intelligent and less spiritual than bodies nearer the Sun. By "spiritual" we mean EN-LIGHT-ENED, or more powerfully charged with the light frequency which carries the "desire" or the "will" of the One Great Light that runs the Cosmos.

Mercury is that orb nearer to the Sun than any other of the planets in our System. It is number One in order. Next in line of distance from our Sun is Venus. The next is planet Earth. Next is Mars, then Jupiter, etc., etc. This would put Venus one planetary Round ahead of us, and the planet Mercury two Rounds in advance of us. Mars, then, would be behind us in spiritual evolution or Enlightenment.

HOW TO SIGHT A "SAUCER". Flying Saucers have been sighted so universally that it is entirely possible that you might be fortunate enough to sight one or more of them in your own vicinity. I would recommend sincerely that you secure for yourself a small telescope, or at least a good pair of binoculars or "opera-glasses". (I never travel without them in my car). Carry them with you on your person every time you go to the nearby hills, desert or beach resort.

My technique for sighting Flying Saucers is basically similar to that used by such notables as George Adamski of Mount Palomar, George Van Tassel of Giant Rock, Truman Bethurum, and others. Here is the essence of the method, which I recommend to you:

1. Get away from large cities. There is so much light and atmospheric disturbance around big cities, it's practically impossible to detect any Saucer phenomena in the skies. Try to spend a full weekend in the country or on the desert. Your chances of sighting a disc will thereby be increased many fold.

2. Don't try to see Spacecraft during mid-day. Sunlight makes them almost invisible. Wait until afternoon or evening or night before scanning the skies. You might even prefer to hold your "Saucer Vigil" all night long, then sleep during the daytime. Remember, they glow at night (often resembling a full moon of reddish orange color) so you will be able to spot them quickly if they should happen to cross the sky in your vicinity.

3. If at all possible, go where the Flying Saucers are reported to have been seen by other people whom you believe to be reliable. This would be primarily the desert areas of California, Arizona, New Mexico etc., as these make the most ideal natural landing places.

4. Form a definite habit of following your inner feelings. Let the gentle voice of Intuition lead you to the proper place where a genuine sighting of a Flying Saucer can be made. Follow all leads.

5. Be persistent. Numerous trips to various localities might be necessary before you are rewarded with the amazing view you are now seeking. On the other hand, YOU may be one of the fortunate individuals who might not only see an interplanetary Spaceship but contact the beings within it also...and all this when you least expect it!

6. Do not be skeptical. This mental attitude cuts you off from the desirable attractive state of mind that is essential to success. Be open-minded. So many sightings are on record now by qualified observers, very little "blind faith" is required. With sightings now increasing instead of decreasing, your chances of personally seeing a "UFO" are getting better and better.

7. Familiarize yourself with the various kinds of sky objects that are most commonly mistaken for Flying Saucers but actually are not. These include (a) Weather balloons, (b) High altitude balloons or "Sky Hooks", (c) New type aircraft, (d) Unusual cloud effects. By knowing what these and other natural sky phenomena look like, you will be able to refute any arguments by "Saucer Critics" who may try to belittle your sightings by claiming you are not "up" on the new developments in Aviation and Science. This information will also enable you to recognize a genuine UFO when you see one. Remember too that the regular habit of looking upward "to the sky" will so strengthen your vision you will be able to see higher and farther.

You have only to see a single one of these amazing Spacecraft to know forevermore that they are not illusion, delusion, nor merely imagination. Nor are they simply "spots before the eyes" as some persons would have us believe. It is my conviction that Flying Saucers do exist and all men will see them in the Golden Age coming. In this monograph I have given you many vital links in the seeming mystery of Flying Saucers. If you follow the suggestions I have given you will be rewarded, in a wonderful way. Be bold. Intuitively, you KNOW flying saucers exist. All that remains is for you to sight one (or several at once) for yourself.

To you then will come a glorious NEW consciousness--an ecstatic feeling of dwelling in two different worlds at one time. This feeling will persist with you for days after your first sighting of an interplanetary craft. As a final closing word now I would remind you that sincere desire is in reality PRAYER. So if you wholeheartedly desire to sight a Flying Saucer, in due time you shall. It may not be tomorrow, but the day will come. When it happens, it will be one of the most thrilling days you've ever known on planet Earth!

Flying Saucers At Giant Rock

by

MICHAEL X

Mystic Monograph No. 2

MYSTIC MONOGRAPH   "FLYING SAUCERS AT GIANT ROCK"   NUMBER TWO

Part One

Out of This World.

    Dr. Nephi Cottam gazed in amazement at the glittering, glowing, silvery thing hovering motionless in the sky above him. He had never seen a space ship before. He was seeing one now, and he knew it.

    The "Saucer" was about two miles above the ground. It had not been there a minute ago. Now, however, it was there and...it was REAL. Nephi had no doubt about that.

    He had spotted the Flying Saucer a few seconds before, when it first appeared. Then it was only a tiny spot of bright light in the far distance; but as he watched in complete fascination, the "light" seemed to hurl itself across the miles of sky until it reached its present position. There it rested quietly above the crowd below.

    Nephi smiled. It was really true. He was seeing a Flying Saucer. It wasn't merely "imagination", nor was it a case of having "spots before the eyes". That bright circular object in the sky was every bit as much of a reality to him as was the light bulb in his bedroom lamp at home. If that light bulb was "real", so was this Saucer. He turned to the man next to him.

    "What does that look like to you?" Nephi asked.

    "Flying Saucer!" the other man said.

    "Yes," Nephi remarked, "It's a Saucer."

    But then, that's exactly what he had been hoping to see. That is what several thousand other people at this meeting had been hoping to see. Now they were happily sighting a ship from another world.

    It was the exciting climax to a never-to-be-forgotten day at Giant Rock Airport in Yucca Valley, California. The date was Sunday, March 12, 1955. The latest interplanetary Spacecraft Convention was going on, and people from all walks of life were on hand for the tremendous occasion.

    George Adamski, author of "Flying Saucers Have Landed", was a guest speaker. So was Frank Scully ("Behind the Flying Saucers"), Orfeo Angelucci and Truman Bethurum--who have been aboard the spaceships--were also there. George W. Van Tassel, author of the startling book, "I Rode a Flying Saucer", was another of the many notable Saucer authorities who were present at the Convention.

    It was late afternoon. Nephi looked up again. The Saucer was still motionless and silent like a flashlight in the sky. There were no clouds to obscure it from view. All you had to do now was look up and you would see it. Those intelligent beings up there certainly knew what was going on down here at the "Rock"; but in spite of the fact that this Convention was "in their honor", they made no attempt to land their glowing Space Ship.

All at once, the Saucer accelerated suddenly, then went straight up higher and higher until finally it was lost to view. The crowd began dispersing, for the "show" was over and tomorrow was a workday. Nephi Cottam returned to his home in Los Angeles.

When I talked with him a month later, the memory of having "sighted" an actual Flying Saucer was still fresh and clear in his mind. Since I had not been able to attend the Spacecraft Convention myself, I got as complete an account of the event as I wanted, from Nephi. I have known the doctor for a number of years. He is the originator of a unique and wonderful method of healing known as "Craniopathy". This is a technique for releasing Brain-Energy by physical and mental means.

Past experience has proven Nephi to be a remarkable individual. Through meditation and intuitive insight, he has gained access to healing knowledge which, if the world knew about it, would largely do away with the need for "going to doctors". The individual would merely apply a sort of "Self-Therapy" and remain ever healthy.

Nephi Cottam was working for the good of mankind, along the lines of Truth. So there was no reason for me to doubt his integrity. All that I needed was more facts.

My personal knowledge of Giant Rock Airport and the men and women who lived at the "Rock" was, at the moment, rather sketchy. I knew only that the "man in charge" at Giant Rock was one George W. Van Tassel. It was my impression that George operated a private Airport there in Yucca Valley, and was a licensed airplane pilot. Also, I was aware that George had written an account of his "contact" with the Space People, and the ride he had in one of their interplanetary "Air Ships". That, in a nutshell, was all I knew about the mysterious activities of "George's Group" at Giant Rock. Remember, I had never been there.

It seemed to me, however, that George Van Tassel was one person who understood some things about Flying Saucers that most people (including yours truly) didn't know. If George was actually in personal contact with the Saucer People, then he logically must have received certain information from them which to us would be tremendously vital. Reasoning along these lines, I concluded that a "Field trip" to Giant Rock was in order. I asked Nephi if he could join me.

"Surely," he replied, "How about leaving Los Angeles at six A. M. on May the 8th?"

"Fine, I agreed. An early start was always a good idea. It was quite a distance out to the desert from the city center. Then too, we planned to return to L.A. in the evening of the same day if all went well.

On Sunday morning, 8 May, we drove to Giant Rock. By taking the Super Highways which had recently been completed between L.A. and San Bernardino, the trip to Yucca Valley--although more than a hundred miles--seemed like a "breeze" to us. Almost before we knew it, the dry desert land was stretching out in front of us. Soon we found ourselves bumping over an unpaved dirt road in the direction of the private Airport. The terrain became more scenic. Instead of uninteresting flat desert, huge rocks and boulders of all sizes lay scattered about.

Nephi pointed to a small sign at an intersection in the road. It read, "Giant Rock Airport". We followed it. Abruptly we came to another sign which said, "George's Gang Welcomes You". Then we saw the "Rock". Several "stories" in height, Giant Rock was aptly named. I sensed the immensity, the strength and majesty of its presence. Although no match in size for the famous Rock of Gibralter, Giant Rock was, for all that, quite a "pebble" in its own right.

As we drove up to the base of the Rock, a man approached in response to my friendly greeting and wave of the hand. He was a well-proportioned, intelligent looking individual. I mentally catalogued him as a sturdy "salt of the earth" Dutchman.

We introductd ourselves, and the man smiled pleasantly. "I'm George Van Tassel" he said. "Make yourselves at home, and I will show you about in a few minutes."

I parked at one side of the Rock. We got out, stretched, then looked around. Not many other people in sight. Maybe a "baker's dozen" or so, including us two. There was, I realized, no "Convention" of any kind going on now. That, in a way, was fortunate for us. There would be no swarming crowds of people all trying to talk to George at the same time. He would have more time to converse with us.

George invited us into one of the few small buildings located close to the Rock. It was designed to serve as a "short-order" Cafe, for the conveniences of visitors. Behind the counter stood a woman, whom George introduced as his wife. The walls of the cafe were covered with photographs and drawings of spaceships of every description. I stepped over to them, noting all details as carefully as possible. One of the pictures showed a great cloud shaped liked a huge bowl, hovering about a half mile above the earth. It was clear that the "cloud" was more than it appeared to be. George explained to us:

"That is actually a Saucer camouflaging itself within its own force field of energy. To our physical eye it looks like a large, swirling cloud."

I glanced quickly at several of the other pictures. A number of them bore the name and copyright notice of George Adamski. There were the well known photos of saucers passing between the earth and the moon, with the moon in the background. Also, telescopic pictures of a giant carrier ship, often called the "mother ship". It was shaped like a cigar. The pictures were amazing.

George seemed interested in us. He began answering some of our questions. When he spoke, you got the impression he was speaking from personal experience. Everything he said fitted together like links in a chain. Nothing seemed to perturb him.

"Are the Saucers interplanetary?" I asked, "Or do they come from some Government on Earth?"

"They come from other planets," George said. "Mainly from Venus. Scientists on Earth have not captured the secret of interstellar travel, which is simply based upon use of FREE Energy. The Space People have found out how to channel that power."

"FREE Energy," I remarked, "Isn't that what Walter Russell was talking about in his book called "The Secret of Light?"

"Yes, there is a very good description of the secondary effects of Light in that book. Light is really the basic Universal Power. It passes constantly through your body, maintaining life. It causes planets to spin, nebulae to evolve, suns to shine, and really runs the whole universe."

Nephi and I both nodded our heads to show that the idea made sense to us. We felt ourselves to be on the verge of some truly tremendous discoveries about Life.

"FREE Energy," continued George, "is Free. That's where the rub comes. Imagine, no more light bills to pay nor gasoline to buy. No more special money interests. All you can use would be free. They can't patent the power that runs the Cosmos! Everyone would be using FREE Energy. It's so simple any good mechanic can make the equipment for utilizing it in a million ways!"

"That would upset our world economy," I commented, "Imagine, no money system!"

"Authorities are trying hard to prevent the inevitable from happening," George said, "That's why they're hiding their findings about Flying Saucers. They are mortally afraid that the public will find out about the FREE Energy that powers the universe!"

It was easy to see that the "FREE Energy" was a bombshell of no little proportions. No wonder the real facts were being kept hidden from the man in the street. The story of Keely's motor flashed to mind. I recalled that John Worrell Keely, a lonely inventor of Philadelphia, Penna., had developed a motor which generated its own power after having once been started. If allowed to continue running it would do so until the bearings wore themselves out!

What happened to Keely's engine? It had one disadvantage. Unless Keely himself was there the engine would not operate. So the money-backers lost interest, and Keely faded into obscurity, a disillusioned man.

Nikola Tesla, the famed wizard of electricity, also stumbled onto the secret of FREE Energy. He built a working model of an engine, to demonstrate a simple form of perpetual motion. Money-interests got wind of it, however, and wrecked his laboratory.

Bell Telephone Company recently developed a "Solar Battery" consisting of a series of flat crystals which store up energy from the sun. Though crude, this is a step in the right direction of FREE Energy.

I do not doubt that the secret will be rediscovered and used again by man to speed his spiritual progress. Occultists are now aware of the basic principle: Intercept the lines of light energy from the sun, and you bring about a rotation movement. This is how planets revolve. Motors do likewise.

"Would you care to see our room under the Rock?" George asked us. We assured him that we would be happy to accompany him there. I had a hunch that much more knowledge was about to be revealed.

* * * * * * *

"FLYING SAUCERS AT GIANT ROCK"

Part Two

"Wisdom of The Cosmos"

It was midafternoon. The desert sky was intensely clear and blue. The air was fresh and exhilarating. Dr. Nephi Cottam and I followed in single file behind George Van Tassel as he walked out of the "Cafe" toward the "Communications Room" underneath Giant Rock.

George opened a door leading down a series of stone steps into the "Room". It was a spacious place, and gave me the eerie feeling of being inside solid rock. The ceiling of the Room, however, consisted of a small portion of the bottom of the Rock. The builders had dug under one edge of the Rock, scraped out space for a room, then built up walls around it.

Other visitors to the Rock--ten or so in number--joined us as we descended the stone stairs into the Room below. Several chairs were available there, so all of us sat down in a semicircle around the main speaker, which of course, was George.

He began speaking, and we listened.

"The scientists of Earth are majoring in the science of destruction, in separation, disintegration and taking things apart. According to the Space People, that is the wrong approach to the mysteries of Creation.

"We, as a people, shall only attain supreme Knowledge and the wisdom of the Cosmos by constructive efforts, by putting things together. Our science is in error.

"Nuclear energy--atomic power--is being used so negatively that our whole planet is endangered. Every explosion brings about a reaction in the lines of force maintaining planetary balance or equilibrium. Each explosion charges our atmosphere with radioactive debris that will remain poisonous for thousands of years.

"The Space People are aware of these dangers and, for the sake of humanity on this planet as well as the life on other worlds, are seeking to nullify the effects."

One of the group had a question: "What do the Space People look like? I heard that they are smaller than we are."

"Yes, they are 'Little People' when they come from a planet with a gravitational density greater than ours," George said.

"On the other hand, many planets have produced beings of our average size. Some Solar Systems beyond ours produce people whom you or I would consider to be giants.

"The teaching of the Church is that there is only a 'here' and a 'hereafter'. Here means of course, the earth. Hereafter refers to Heaven or to Purgatory, a place where souls wait to be let into Heaven. All such dogma is wrong because it seeks to limit the Creator. It tries to confine God to only two life levels, whereas the fact is that people are coming to our level (Earth) in spacecraft from many different levels throughout the Cosmos.

"'In my Father's House are many mansions', Jesus reminded us. Substitute the word 'planets' for 'mansions' and you get a much clearer picture of what he meant.

"Visitors from space have told us that they have found human life everywhere. On many planets in other Solar Systems the people are advanced so far beyond us earthlings in Culture and Science, it staggers the imagination. We of Earth simply can't comprehend how anybody could be more 'advanced' and 'intelligent' than we are.

"But what are the facts? Is not the whole economy of the nations of Earth based on manufacturing weapons of destruction, planes, jets, guided missiles, battleships, tanks, and atomic or hydrogen bombs? Take away the iron fist of the Military and the nation would, supposedly, be doomed."

At this point George paused briefly. He seemed to be waiting for another question from the group. I gave him one.

"Why are the Saucers coming to our Earth?" I asked, "Is something big impending?"

I had known for some time that Flying Saucers have been landing on Earth in continually greater numbers. What did this mean? What did the Saucer People want? I felt that George might supply the key.

"A planetary cataclysm of Terra (the Earth) has been foreseen by the Space People," George said. "At the present time we are not only on the pinnacle of a Minor Cycle, which is approximately every 2100 years, but are also in the middle of a Major or Master Cycle (about 26,000 years) at the same time. This brings about a balancing of the planetary forces.

"In the Christian Bible this is called the time of the great earthquake, or the 'shaking terribly' of the earth. (For the full story, see Monograph No. 5.)

"According to the Space People, that is the time when a 'polar flip' will occur, due to the gyroscopic action of the earth. When this event takes place, many of Earth's inhabitants will be taken out of physical embodiment. These will be the mass-minded who have no interest in matters of a spiritual or cosmic nature.

"The other people of Earth--those who have diligently sought the 'Light' and endeavored to become better human beings--will be taken up in Flying Saucers by the Space People, and protected by them until the planetary catastrophe is over.

"Then," continued George, "the 'elect' will be returned to Earth to bring in the Millenium, the thousand years of peace."

This, I recalled, tied in with the Biblical prophecies of the 'last days' in which John foretold of a "new heaven and a new Earth". This new Earth would be under the law of the spirit, which is the "New Dispensation" mankind has long awaited. "And God shall wipe away all tears from their eyes; and there shall be no more death, neither sorrow, nor crying, neither shall there be any more pain: for the former things are passed away." (Rev. Chapter 21:4)

The idea of our Earth making a sudden 'shift' of its axis at periodic intervals, has long been known to Occultists. Those who study the ancient teachings of man--the Ageless Wisdom--have long been aware of "Cataclysmic Cycles" which occur regularly in the history of most planets.

There is, in fact, a definite pattern of periodic "destruction", which is Nature's own doing. As you know, each planet begins its human life expression with what is called a "Root Race". Each Root Race lasts for about 5 million years, then is almost completely annihilated by either water or fire. Then the next Root Race begins, from a small nucleus of persons who were spared.

It is said that each planet of our Solar System is allowed to have 7 Root Races. (I am not speaking now of the white race, colored race, yellow race, etc., but rather the Race of Man itself). We of this day and age are members of the 5th Root Race.

Root races of odd number are subject to destruction by fire. This, in modern times could mean not only physical fire as we know it, but could include the Hydrogen Bomb which creates a holocaust of flames. Strangely enough, if we look backwards for a moment to note how the previous Root Races perished, we see the following: The first Root Race--the Adamic--was cut in two by a "fiery sword", which drove Adam and Eve out of the Garden of Eden. This "fiery sword" was in reality a fiery comet that approached too close to planet Earth and became drawn into our terrestial atmosphere. The comet with its "tail of fire" looked much like a burning sword of vengeance.

The second Root Race (a Sub-Race of the first) was undoubtedly the Noaic Race, or Noah and his people. As you realize, most of the human race in the time of Noah were a bad lot, having lost sight of their own spiritual heritage. Noah, of course, was the exception; hence he and his faithful followers were spared when the Deluge came.

Ancient writings tell us that Lemuria became the third Root Race after the Deluge. Volcanic disturbances of the Earth caused such upheavals of the oceans that the continent of Lemuria was swept over by the Pacific Ocean...wiping out most of the Race.

The Fourth Race Atlanteans, we learn, met a watery fate at the bottom of the Atlantic.

According to the Great Pyramid, we are now living in the Saturday Night of Time. It is, actually, the beginning of the "Time of the End" for humankind on Earth. This means that some collossal changes are due to take place before January 1, 2,000 A.D.

There is, however, no need for panic. So far as you and I are concerned, there is no doubt that we shall be advised as to the proper "protective action" to take, long in advance of any such Cataclysm as we have described. As long as we remain loyal "Seekers of the True Light" we need never be frightened by anything that might happen on Earth. In other words, the quality of our thought IS our protection. Good thought, plus good feeling can build strong armour.

Noah, you remember, was warned many years before the Great Flood happened. As a result of his "advance information" Noah was in a position to prepare for what was to come. We should then, cast out all fear or terror from our hearts, and live more and more from "the Spirit"--from the Great God-Presence within us.

While all of us had been relaxing, George was setting up a tape-recorder on a small table in the center of the room. He was now ready to play-back one of the tapes for us to listen to. These contained "messages from outer space" which had been received telepathically by George Van Tassel. It was interesting to learn how this was done. A powerful beam of light was focussed by the Space People (who were in a giant Carrier Ship, positioned on a special "Space Station" 800 miles above the earth) upon George who acted as "receiver". The mind vibrations or "thoughts" of the Space Men were transmitted through this light--which was known as the "Omni-Beam"--in the form of mental images. George then made a "vocal translation" of the ideas he received, and spoke them onto the magnetic tape.

"This first message", he informed us, "was received by us on April 16th, of this year. It is from an individual by the name of Desca. The amazing thing here is that we received this information concerning the harmful effects of the "Polio Vaccine" several weeks before the authorities learned of its danger and withdrew the Vaccine from the general public. Here is the message:

"As most of you know, one of the Ten Commandments states, 'Thou shalt not commit adultery!' In the twisting of words and meanings this has come to be believed in as the violation of marriage laws; human marriage laws of civil origin. This law could have read, 'Thou shalt not commit DILUTION.' The adulteration of anything is the mixing of anything else with it.

"Your propaganda machines there have carried information about the new Polio Vaccine. Whatever it be that is injected into the bloodstream is DILUTION and violation of the commandment, 'Thou shalt not adulterate thyself!'

"The blood is the life of the physical body. Adulteration of the blood changes the frequency, the vibratory rate, and can be the cause of obsession, mental failure, and nerve failure. The blood is the result of a series of chemical-electrical changes in the laboratory of the body. Sudden additions of anything to the bloodstream may, in some cases, bring about a prevention of some particular disease; but the effect of injections of any chemical into the bloodstream will, sooner or later, cause REACTION that will be of a more deadly potential than the original disease could have been. If these Vaccines could be assimilated very gradually over a long period of time the body chemistry could adjust itself to them.

"The new Polio Vaccine (Salk) has not been sufficiently tested for a period of time that would determine conditions that will be apparent in the near future. The ignorance in medicine upon the Earth is in assuming that every individual responds equally to the same application. This will be proven in many ways. The present formula for Polio Vaccine will cause an increase in heart failure, tuberculosis, spinal meningitus, dropsy, and other numerous kidney ailments, and in the long run will bring about an unbalanced mental condition."

Desca's foresight was proven accurate when our Government suddenly clamped down on distribution of the Vaccine in the U. S. Restrictions now, have been made more stringent as regards making of the Vaccine; but nearly a hundred deaths in our nation could be traced to use of the Vaccine at that time.

The next message was extremely fascinating. It was received, George explained, from a planet outside of our Solar System. I shall not try to recall the entire message verbatim. However, the gist of it was that the people on that planet were 400,000 years ahead of us Earthlings in scientific and cultural development.

The geography of their land was flat, whereas our Earth has mountains and hills. All homes and factories on their planet were dome-shaped and made of a translucent material. Machinery, powered by FREE Energy (Magnetic Light-Power) did most of the work, under the watchful eyes of one or two men instead of many men.

Children were educated at home by the parents, who taught by Audio-Visual means, from data issued from a central source. It was considered unnecessary for anyone on that highly evolved planet to use "words" in communicating ideas to each other. Instead, a method of mental telepathy, called "Telethot" was used by the vast majority. For this reason, most of the dwellers of that planet could not speak. As they see it, the mouth was made to eat with, and the brain or rather mind was made to speak with. However, at least one individual in every family was taught to speak in sounds as we do.

After the above mentioned message was heard by our group, George indicated that he expected to have more tape-recorded messages by the next weekend. All who so wished were welcome to return then and hear them.

Nephi and I arose. It was time to be on our way back to the big city. Stepping over to the chair where George was seated, we bid him farewell and thanked him heartily for all his illuminating discourses.

He smiled and shook our hands in a wonderful feeling of love and kinship. We turned and walked up the stone stairs to the door which opened to the desert. Outside, the air was bracing. Pausing briefly, Nephi and I inhaled deeply. This visit to Giant Rock had been a most memorable experience. Much new and vitally important data had been presented to us here. For one thing, our concept of the universe had been expanded tremendously. Now we saw God's universe as a creation of vast and magnificent proportions, with not just two life levels to consider, but a universe with myriads of intelligences of varying levels of life. Suns beyond suns. Planets beyond planets. Solar systems beyond solar systems. Yes, even worlds within worlds...and our Earth but a speck in this mighty universe!

Yet every single electron in an atom is important to the perfect functioning of that atom. Likewise planet Earth is important in the smooth working of the Creator's Master Plan. We are, you and I, in a kindergarten as it were. Our goal is spiritual evolution into a more perfect expression of Life, Love and Light. But we can grow up and out of "kindergarten" if we put our minds to it, just as we grew out of lower grades in school and advanced to the higher grades. If we do this with a conscious will and desire, we'll make much faster progress on the UPWARD PATH leading to the PERFECTED MAN AND WOMAN.

Then, at the proper time, we'll be invited to enjoy a new and thrilling life on a more highly evolved planet than Earth. And, as much as we love Earth, we'll know that our next step upward will be to an even more ideal world than we have known here. We'll realize that ALL WORLDS are essential units in the great design, and each is worthy of our love and our understanding heart.

Yes, this visit with George Van Tassel had filled our minds with many vital new thoughts. The coming gyroscopic SHIFT of the Earth, the amazing concept of FREE Energy, and the idea that some of the inhabitants of other planets possess culture and intelligence that may be millions of years in advance of ours...Nephi and I looked at each other and smiled. Both of us felt raised in consciousness. It could well be that this was only the "beginning" of the many glorious adventures which awaited us with the Space People themselves.

We got into our car and pointed it in the direction of Los Angeles. As we drove away, we knew we would remember Giant Rock!

oooOOOooo

Secrets Of The Saucer People

by

MICHAEL X

Mystic Monograph No. 3

MYSTIC MONOGRAPHS   NUMBER THREE

"SECRETS OF THE SAUCER PEOPLE"

Part One

The Venusian

Several weeks had passed since my eventful trip to Giant Rock (See Mystic Monograph No. 2, "Flying Saucers at Giant Rock") and as yet I had not been privileged to personally contact any of Earth's "Interplanetary Guests".

I was, however, hopeful. When the time was appropriate for me to meet the Saucer People, the meeting would come about in as natural and normal a manner as possible. I knew that it was up to me to take the "first step". How that was to be done I was not at all sure. So I meditated on the problem.

The answer came sooner than I expected. It was so simple as to seem almost childish. Here is the direction I received, as to how I should communicate with the Saucer People:

We live in a mental universe. That is, all space is filled with "mind-stuff" or Ether which can transmit mental vibrations, in the same manner that it transmits radio waves from the Broadcasting Station to your receiving set (radio) at home.

Occultists know that by utilizing the personal energy known as "Vril" it is possible to raise the personal vibrations to an ultra-high frequency or speed. Thought vibrations may then be conveyed on that high frequency to any region in our Solar System.

As most students of esoteric science realize, there are SEVEN ETHERS. Later on, we shall study these Ethers more closely. Four of these Ethers are called, respectively,

(1) The Chemical Ether
(2) The Life Ether (Prana)
(3) The Light Ether
(4) The Reflecting Ether

The final three Ethers (5, 6, & 7) are of such a sacred, spiritual nature that only the highest Adepts are permitted to utilize them for mystical and occult purposes. For purposes of contacting the Saucer People, one need only make use of the Light Ether. The reason for this is that they are "Beings of Light" in the fullest sense of the word.

If you wish to listen to a particular radio program on your radio, you must "tune in" to the proper wave-length or frequency. Otherwise you would get a "scramble" of all the various radio programs...that is, you'd pick up portions of different programs as you turned the tuning dial. Only by turning to the right station could you expect to receive the message you desire to hear.

The Saucer People communicate by THINKING ON THE WAVE-LENGTH OF LIGHT. That means we must use the LIGHT ETHER to contact them, as well as to receive messages from them. Ordinary "radio-waves" are transmitted through the Reflecting Ether, NOT the Light Ether. We are concerned only with use of this Light Ether for transmitting THOUGHTS.

So fascinating is this subject of the Seven Ethers, I could write for hours about them and their great importance to us all. That, however, I shall have to leave for another Monograph at some future time. At this point, I believe you would be interested in knowing the details of my unique method of communicating with another world.

On any clear night, look up at the sky and you will quickly see Venus, for it is the brightest star in the sky. Some people call it the "Evening Star"; others refer to it as the "Morning Star", for it is easily visible at both night and morning.

I had long believed that mental communication between planets was not only possible but that it would someday become almost as simple as our "long-distance" phone calls. So I set about the business of attempting to reach the planet Venus by means of Telepathy.

On the night of May 22, 1955, I gazed up at Venus and projected a vibratory "beam of light" from the center of my forehead to the mysterious planet whose influence upon Earth is far greater than humanity can imagine. In the words of the ancient book, "The Commentary", Venus is our Earth's spiritual "prototype". Every sin committed on Earth is felt by Venus", says the Commentary. "She is the Guardian Spirit of the Earth and men. Every change on Venus is felt on and reflected by the Earth.

"Every world has its 'parent star' and 'sister planet'," continues the Commentary. "The Earth is the adopted child and younger brother of Venus, but its inhabitants are of their own kind...all sentient (conscious) complete beings are furnished, in their beginnings, with forms and organizms in full harmony with the nature and states of the sphere they inhabit." It was in line with these ancient teachings that I looked upon Venus as being Earth's teacher.

I was, during this attempt at "space telepathy", comfortably positioned on the roof of my house. There I was least liable to disturbance while concentrating. Also, it was quiet and dark so that I had no difficulty in focussing my thoughts. The message I decided to "transmit" to Venus was this:

"MICHAEL OF EARTH CALLING VENUS. COME IN VENUS. COME IN VENUS. OVER."

This is the established "form" of communication language used by all Airline pilots on Earth. It is standard radio practice. I was, of course, not at all sure that interplanetary beings referred to their own planet as "Venus" or to ours as "Earth". There would be, however, a mutual "meeting of the minds" as to what I meant. This I was sure of, since I would "transmit" in the form of Mind Images and Pictures rather than words.

It was 10:00 P.M. For nearly one half-hour I concentrated on sending my message. I would transmit my thought for 5 minutes, then wait receptively for 5 minutes. There was no response. At about 10:30 P.M. I gave the whole thing up for the night and dozed off to sleep on a cot which I had hauled up to the rooftop for this special purpose.

At 2:00 A.M. an amazing thing happened. A voice was calling my name. "MICHAEL, MICHAEL..." It kept saying, in penetrating, melodious tones. It was an extremely beautiful voice, clear and bell-like. Instinctively, I opened my eyes. No other human being was in sight. I was entirely alone on my cot in the darkness and only the stars and the shimmering moon were visible.

A vivid dream, I thought to myself as I closed my eyes to resume sleeping. Then I knew this was not a dream but a reality. A voice was speaking to me slowly and distinctly, repeating my name. I responded by means of Mental Telepathy as best I could.

"Who are you?" was all I could think to say, for I still thought it possible that my mind might be "playing tricks" on me.

"I am a human being, much like yourself." The voice replied, after what seemed like a delay of nearly a full minute. "My planet is the one you call 'Venus'. We have intercepted your communication by Telethot, and are pleased to make this contact with you."

The voice of the Venusian continued: "We have known of your work along the lines of Occult Science," he said, "and consider it good. You and your companions are moving in the right direction. It is our purpose to guide you, from time to time, without superimposing our will upon yours. I am not at liberty to reveal certain details in regard to this planet; but questions of a general nature can be answered freely by us."

"Tell me something of your science and culture." I inquired, "Also, what is your means of power for interplanetary flight?"

"We are nearing the middle of our 7th Planetary Round", replied the Venusian. "You people of Terra (Earth) are in the midst of your 4th Round. In simple terms, this means we are nearly fifteen million years ahead of your planet in respect to global evolution. As you know, every planet begins its life in an etheric condition. Gradually, after several millions of years, it evolves into a sphere of physical matter that is hard and condensed. Still later, when the planet reaches its final Round, there is a reversal of the trend. It returns again to its original state of soft, etheric matter.

"Consider a baby on your Earth;" said the Venusian, "At birth the baby's body and bone structure are extremely soft, pliable and almost 'fluid' in consistency. As the body matures, the bones harden and become more brittle. The entire form becomes toughen and appears more solid and lasting.

"Planets too, are bodies. They are also 'beings' on their own life level, having an evolutionary path of their own to follow.

"It is almost beyond the comprehension of Earth beings to grasp the tremendous Knowledge that our people of 'Venus' have attained down through the milleniums of Time.

"Perhaps the first fact you should become aware of, insofar as we Venusians are concerned, is that all of our people have long ago discovered their correct relationship with the 'Father' of the Cosmic Universe in which we are living. We know and use as a working principle, the immense power of the Creator's Will which is expressed through the action of physical light in all Galactic Universes."

There was a long pause. Apparently the speaker desired his last thought to "sink in" for it was five minutes before his next idea came spinning across the thousands of miles between himself and me.

The next thing he said was, "Michael, am I clear? Are you getting tired?"

I immediately replied that I was not tired and that I was receiving his thought clearly, and would he please continue?

"The 'will' of the Creator is eternally active in all his creations," explained my Venusian teacher. "His 'will' works through Man, by means of the 'light' whithin that 'lighteth every man that cometh into the world'. This is the positive or spiritual power in Conscious Man and Woman.

"The Mystic purpose of all created human intelligences is to actively express love, which is the stabilizing power that harmonizes the impelling power of 'will'. This brings about a balance---and is the primary law of the entire Cosmos."

As he said these things, I found myself unconsciously 'linking' them up with one of Christ's mysterious expressions, "The Father works, and I work". Everything in the Cosmos was seeking fulfillment --balance--rest.

"What you call 'motion' is the natural result of a universal need in all material things, to achieve a condition of balance. It is through 'voiding' certain opposing forces, that all things are able to move. When the resisting energies have been fully 'voided', motion then ceases automatically."

To the Venusian, the ideas he was presenting were "elementary" but to my mind they seemed at least slightly "bewildering". He had an entirely different way of thinking and as yet I was not prepared for it. His mind thought in terms of PRIMARY CAUSES, all based on Cosmic laws, which are entirely TRUE in essence. We of Earth, for the most part, are not centered in true cause, but are "off-centered" in EFFECTS. In other words, we know HOW many things happen, but we haven't the slightest idea WHY they happen.

For several days prior to my "telephone" contact with a being from another world, I had been making up a "list" of questions to ask such a being. As you of course realize, certain questions which deal with matters beyond our immediate scope of interest, or which are considered "restricted" by the Space People, were not included in the list.

However, I did include a great variety of questions. Most of them are direct and simple. Some were complex and deep. When the Venusian mind-waves reached mine, these are some of the questions I asked and the answers I was given by my instructor:

QUESTION: "What do your people (The Venusians) look like?

ANSWER: "Venusians are of two sexes, male and female, as on your planet. Many of our Adepts are androgynous, having both masculine and feminine polarities perfectly balanced in the physical body. Our facial features are somewhat different, being smoother and broader, especially the forehead. Centuries of mental telepathy have produced our characteristics in this respect."

QUESTION: "Physically, then, you resemble to a considerable extent, a 'humanoid'?"

ANSWER: "Yes. Our average height is 5'-7". However, there is a difference in bodily weight and structure as compared with Earthlings. If you should come to our planet you would weigh slightly more than you do on Earth, to compensate for the fact that our planet is only 80% as large in mass as your Earth. Our bodies are more etheric, in keeping with the evolutionary stage of our planet and are therefore lighter in weight than yours. The atomic structure is less dense and the radiation of the 'light within' is greater, ennabling us to appear young and beautiful at a much greater age than you of Earth are yet able to appear. The humanoid form is found on almost every habitable planet in space. The big difference between planets is largely in the mental and spiritual development achieved."

* * * * *

"SECRETS OF THE SAUCER PEOPLE"

Part Two

Secrets of The Universe

QUESTION: "Do the 'visitors' from outer space all come from your planet Venus?"

ANSWER: "Most of the Space People who have landed on Earth do come from Venus; many are from Mars. A great many extra-terrestial visitors also have come from other densities in the Cosmos. Some have even come from other Solar systems than ours. They were on exploratory flights."

Q: "Is interplanetary flight as dangerous and difficult as it appears to be?"

A: "This depends. If you try to conquer space with 'rocket-power' or 'atomic engines' it would be utterly disastrous. A space flight powered by FREE Energy would be an entirely different matter. You would be sure of getting to your destination because you could depend on never running out of fuel since it is available in all parts of this Solar System. More important, by using FREE Energy, you would be able to get back to the original point of departure. Space People have been flying between planets for thousands and thousands of years. To us it is essentially a simple matter, and it is extremely rare that any of our ships are lost through space accidents.

Q: "Such accidents do occur?"

A: "Yes, though infrequently. As long as our space navigators stay within the vortex of this particular Solar System, little danger exists. It is when flights are made between separate universes that miscalculations may be made."

Q: What do you mean by 'vortex'?"

A: "A vortex is an energy field which has the shape of a whirlpool or spiral. In our universe, the Sun radiates the 'Master Vortex'. This produces lines of magnetic force extending to the outermost ends of this Solar System. Within the Master Vortex is the sub-vortex of Mercury, Venus, Earth, Mars, Jupiter, Saturn, and so on. All of these small vortices within the Sun's vortex are known as the 'Great Serpent', or the 'Solar Phalanx'. Space navigators as a rule stay inside of the Solar Phalanx."

Q: "How do Flying Saucers fly?"

A: "I assume you mean our Space Discs. We also call them 'Fire-Ships", because of their glowing, fiery appearance in operation. The means of propulsion is simple enough to understand IF you first grasp the principle of the 'Master Vortex'. A space Disc moves through space by generating a small vortex of its own, within the ship. This vortex of energy is a miniature 'force field'. It is produced and sustained by the great vortex of the Sun itself. When we extend this force field outside of the Space Disc, its lines of magnetic force cut across the primary lines of the Sun's Master Vortex. The effect of this is brilliant, glowing light. Also, the Space Disc instantly goes into motion, following the lines of the Great Vortex. It is trying to 'void' itself by moving from the negative phase of the Vortex to the positive."

Q: "How can the Saucer People remain alive inside a Space Disc, if the Disc becomes a glowing, fiery light?"

A: "There is an opposite polarity between the outside of the Disc and the inside. This creates the effect of hot light on the outer surface or 'skin', and gives a reverse effect of 'cold light' on the inside surface. To simplify this in your mind, you need to know that force always moves--not in straight lines--but in circles, so that it always returns to itself. Within our Spacecraft, cold is opposing heat so we remain cool instead of being as you say, 'cremated'."

B: "What does the surface of Venus look like? Is it hot, 'sand-blasted--that planet that our astronomers think it is?"

A: "No. The scientists of Earth are quite mistaken about that. Venus is extremely verdant and luxuriant with vegetation. It has, however, a predominant blue color whereas on Earth the leaf color is green. Our atmosphere is heavier than that of Earth, so we are protected from excessive sunlight. Because your scientists could not see through our atmosphere, they assumed the worst."

Q: "What causes the rotation of the planets?"

A: "Each planet is surrounded by its own smaller 'Sub-Vortex' or force-field. This field is operative within the larger field of the Sun. As a result, it intercepts the lines of force of the Master Vortex--causing the planet to manifest MOTION in an effort to escape from an unbalanced energy condition. So the sphere rotates."

Q: "Is that a form of perpetual motion, or FREE Energy?"

A: "Yes, it is FREE Energy, or the power that runs the universe we live in."

Q: "Is there a simple key to use in order to understand HOW this FREE Energy works?"

A: "The secret lies simply in gaining a basic 'working knowledge' of Vortexya---that is, the principles of Vortices."

Q: "Do the Venusian people utilize FREE Energy in other ways, besides propelling their Spacecraft by means of it?"

A: "Yes, nearly all the advanced intelligences of the space worlds make use of the universal power of Vortexya in countless practical ways. We use Free Energy to run our factories, light our dwellings, propel our vehicles, and perform a million other necessary services for us. For instance, in our homes it produces light without the need for any containing globes whatsoever."

Q: "Will you explain the method? As you know, we on Earth use light bulbs which have the air extracted from them so that a wire filament can burn or glow within the vacuum, thus producing electric light. Do you have a simpler method of creating light?"

A: "Indeed we have. There is no need for 'wires' or 'bulbs' or vacuum conditions when you cross magnetic lines of force at right angles. That produces the same kind of light as the 'daylight' of nature. It is the Light Ether manifesting itself visibly. We Venusians use this natural form of light in all of our buildings, which, incidentally, are semi-spherical inshape, and formed of a hard, translucent type of plastic."

Q: "Can you tell me why your Space People are coming to this Earth, and what they desire of me and my fellow beings?"

A: "We come to guide Mankind on Earth into the more harmonious, spiritual life. Our purpose is to show Earthlings the secret of all evolution into a higher, grander form of expression and awareness. We are here to inspire Man to a complete dedication of self to the purposes of the Creator. This is in truth the Great Work to which many are called but few are chosen. Your mind is God's mind, whether you realize it or not; for there is but one Mind in the Cosmos. When you consciously know that, you begin to serve the higher Ideals which your spirit knows."

Q: "What is God's 'will' for Man?"

A: "More Life, Love, Truth, and Beauty."

Q: "Does the universe have a lesson to teach Mankind? As you know, we humans are often fearful, anxious and despondent."

A: "Yes. The universe teaches us to seek the 'centre' of peace and harmony within is, and regulate our lives from this one centre. That is how the life of the entire universe with all its planets and suns and stars is regulated. What beauty resides at the centre of things --what order--system! While the great machinery of life goes on throughout the vast Macrocosm, here at the starting-point of all is peace. Here unending harmony abides, a repose which no calamity can disturb. Worlds may end, terrible disasters may happen, wars may be fought and earthquakes shake the face of planets. But still the universe MOVES FORWARD. The pulse of life never stops, the centre remains unhurt. Man needs this calm SERENITY."

Q: "Do you suffer from Diseases of any kind of Venus, or during space flights?

A: "Our people have long since learned the 'inner' causes of disease, and are aware that destructive thoughts or negative emotions (fear, hatred, jealousy, resentment, revenge, etc.) cause an unbalanced physical condition. Why? Because they cause a state of 'contraction' in all of the bodily cells. On the other hand constructive and harmonious thoughts produce E-X-P-A-N-S-I-O-N in all the cells. We realize that contraction is death and expansion is life. So we choose to expand into continually greater L I F E.

"Space flights no longer cause us any physical difficulty. This is because our Spacecraft produces its own 'synthetic gravity' during flight, and also produces its own air of the proper warmth and density.

"The external cold of outer space cannot hurt us, since we utilize the principles of Navaz or Night-Side forces to maintain healthful and comfortable living conditions inside our Spacecraft."

Q: "What do you mean by 'Navaz'?"

A: "That is our term for the Night-Side of Nature. This refers to the circular progression of the forces of the Vortex from the Sun. The lines of force follow a circular path out from the Sun and then return again. Moving from the Sun they belong to the 'Light-Side' of Nature; but when moving back to the Sun they belong to Navaz or the 'Night-Side'."

"Scientists on Earth know practically nothing of the forces found in the Night-Side of Nature. When they do discover these subtle forces, they will have the secret of 'repulsion by levitation'... as well as other secrets Man on Earth has not even imagined. Neither Earth, air, the depth of the seas nor those of interstellar space will hold secrets from that man who approaches from the Godward side to gain knowledge of Navaz."

Q: "Do you require any special kind of food to sustain you on long flights from one planet to another?"

A: "For space travel purposes, we take along with us a concentrated type of food resembling a round, flat wafer. On Venus, these wafers have been subjected to a mind-wave process we call 'Thought-conditioning'. The effect of this is to give the wafer whatever special food taste we desire to enjoy. For example, if we are hungry for a certain 'favorite' food we merely think of that and the wafer will taste like that food. An Earthling, for instance, might think of 'roast beef' or 'fried chicken' and upon eating the wafers would experience precisely the 'taste' reaction in his sensory nerves that he would if he were enjoying the real thing."

Q: "What effects are resulting in the universe from the series of atomic blasts we have been setting off on Earth?"

A: "Atomic nuclear explosions on your planet Earth are a most serious matter. Far more so than your scientists realize. Each explosion disrupts the etheric levels of life such as Atmospherea and Etherea. (See Monograph #4, "The Magic of Ether Ships") That is another reason why Space Ships are landing on Earth in constantly greater numbers. We seek to prevent this kind of destructiveness."

Q: "How do you accomplish your mental and scientific 'miracles'? I have heard the Space People have learned to forestall physical death for centuries. Could you give me and my friends some 'hint' as to your advanced techniques?"

A: "Yes, I can. We have attained mastery of the universal forces unknown to your Earth scientists. Indeed, they can never hope to discover these subtle powers because they are approaching them from the side of the 'physical eye' instead of from the side of the 'spiritual eye'. In the realm beyond magnetism are yet other forces, superior and more intense in vibratory frequency. These forces are operatid BY THE MIND. Mind is of the Creator, and is the sustaining, creating source of everything that exists. An Adept learns how to raise personal vibration up to the higher levels of 'Odic' or Mind-Force. This has sometimes been referred to as 'Vril' and is a wonderful power to acquire. By its use we can almost instantly re-create the cells of the physical body...all this being done by the conscious direction of THOUGHT. With 'Vril' a human being is enabled to retain his or her physical body for a life span of from 300 to 1500 years."

As the Venusian's reply reached me, I suddenly noticed a feeling of complete weariness which seemed to overpower me. This was due, no doubt, to the length of time we had been in 'communication' by Telethot.

Sadly I brought our conversation to an end, after being assured by him that there would be further 'conversations' in the near future. "There is more to talk about," the Space Master said, "and more to learn." A few parting instructions were given to me then, as to how and when the next telethot communication should take place. Then the conversation broke off and I fell into a deep sleep that lasted for many hours.

For days after the communication I felt glorious. That sense of "living" in a great universe of light--electro-magnetic waves of light, wherein 'all things are possible'--became constantly more real to me. I thought of you, dear friend, who would read of that experience in the pages of this Monograph. And I saw you...moving ever Onward, Upward, and Godward...to the highest Realms of Mystic Light with the "Elect" of Mankind.

The Magic Of Ether Ships

by

MICHAEL X

Mystic Monograph No. 4

MYSTIC MONOGRAPH   NUMBER FOUR

"THE MAGIC OF ETHER SHIPS"

Part One

The Etheric Worlds

Suppose--just for a moment--that you had "passed out of the physical embodiment" and are now "dead". No...don't shudder at the thought of physical death. You, as a good student of the deeper mysteries of life, need't have the slightest feeling of fear or anxiety in regard to your "transition". Knowledge and love enable us to cast out even the age-old inherited fear of experiencing so-called "death". So we intend to continually gain a more complete picture of that human episode known as death. The more we learn of the subtle or "occult" side of things, the less use we have for fear.

Going back to our original idea, that quite suddenly you "gave up the ghost" and died...what do you think you would see? That is, what would your spirit--the immortal part of you--what would it see on the "other side" of Life's mystic curtain? If your mind is somewhat dim on that question, be of good cheer and read on, for it IS a mighty big question, and one that has been baffling mortal man for centuries.

In the pages you are now reading, some fascinating new data will be presented to you, which we trust will throw some needed light on this subject of human "life levels". Most of this new information has been given to us by the Space People, through various contacts with humans on Earth. Some of these contacts have been made in recent times by such individuals as George Adamski, George Van Tassel, Truman Bethurum, Orfeo Angelucci and many others too numerous to mention.

To each of these Earthlings has been given information of a dimensionally greater universe than any of us have been aware of before. Now, however, with this new data that has come to us from the Space People, we are getting answers to vital questions.

In 1882, long before the people of our planet had even heard of "Flying Saucers", a man by the name of John Ballou Newbrough received a psychic communication from one of the Space People. This intelligent Being from another world, told John Newbrough that he must write a book by "remote control". That is, the Space Master would dictate the book, and John would transcribe it onto paper, after receiving the message.

Back in those early days, the typewriter had just been invented and was quite a crude affair in comparison to 1955 models. Nevertheless, the Space Master instructed John to purchase a typewriter and to merely hold his hands over the keys each morning an hour before dawn. John did so and found to his utter amazement that his hands typed out the thoughts of the Space Master automatically, without his conscious control. He was told, incidentally, that he was NOT to read what he was writing until the manuscript was completed.

At the end of one year, the immense project had been completed ...all 891 pages of it. And he was instructed to publish it under the title of "OAHSPE", a New Bible. This book was not, mind you, intended to make our Christian Bible "obsolete" in any respect. Rather it was intended to supplement all the former Bibles, Vedas and other sacred books...and to show how all the former bibles are all parts of one stupendous plan of our Heavenly Creator for bringing light to earthly mortals, even as you and I.

The big thing we are interested in at this moment is the unique fact that OAHSPE was written by means of "Telethot" communication between an Earthling and a wise being from another time-space dimension. So when we read OAHSPE we know how it feels to view life, the creation on Earth, the higher spiritual worlds, etc., THROUGH THE EYES OF ONE OF THE SPACE PEOPLE!

Please do not misunderstand me. I am not trying to "sell" the book OAHSPE, for that is not my publication. My object is simply to call your attention to OAHSPE insofar as it relates to Flying Discs and our greater knowledge of the "Other Worlds".

Most public libraries have a copy of OAHSPE that you can secure in case you are interested in further "research" into its revelations. Or, it can be obtained by writing to The Essenes of Kosmon, Rt. 2, Box 26-A, Montrose, Colorado. Such books as OAHSPE (Meaning Sky, Earth and Spirit) are given mankind but once each 3,000 years. It gives light on Man's origin, purpose and destiny; the history of the planet, of the human races, of every major religion. Price of the book is $5.00 postpaid.

In regard to these "Other Worlds" we mentioned a moment ago, we refer to the Etheric Worlds. Sometimes these are called "planes". They are actual worlds of finer physical matter known as "etheric matter". Though you and I cannot see these etheric worlds with the normal physical eye, they CAN be seen by our "inner" or spiritual eye.

There are just TWO Etheric worlds. They are spherical in shape just as our Earth is. And they interpenetrate and surround the Earth. Of course, the average "man in the street" hasn't the slightest inkling of the fact that these two invisible worlds are passing right through him at all times.

It is only when that person "dies" that his spiritual eye wakes up and sees those Etheric Realms. Quite naturally, he is, to say the least, startled by the sight. It is all so completely "strange" to him that he is totally unprepared to function like a good "spirit" should. The Space People tell us that countless millions of souls remain on the lower levels of the spirit-world for hundreds of years.

They have never learned of the existence of the HIGHER HEAVEN WORLDS and so they make no effort to go up higher.

This is deplorable. However, it is not in the least necessary for a human soul to tolerate undue hardship on any level of life. You can, for example, raise your own living standard simply by positive thinking and a determined will. There will always be those who "gravitate" to the "flop-house" environment simply because they think "in reverse".

There are, then, actually THREE WORLDS IN ONE. The physical Earth, and the other two, "intermeshing" Etheric worlds. These last two worlds are known as "Atmospherea" and "Etherea". If you will please note the diagram on the front page of this Monograph you will gain a clearer picture of these invisible worlds. Notice that Atmospherea extends upward from the Earth's surface, and into the high stratosphere several miles above the Earth.

Atmospherea consists of much denser "etheric matter" than is found in Etherea. That is why Atmospherea is the first Density you and I and all mortals will "visit" when and IF we should happen to pass out of physical embodiment. However, since there are certain methods and practices we can follow to keep our physical bodies in vital "balance" at all times, there is absolutely no need to "shuffle off this mortal coil" by dying. As you may recall, few of the true ADEPTS of history ever gave up their physical body.

Instead, they perfected the physical by refining the atomic structures of the cells. Enoch, you will remember, did not go through the experience of death. He "walked with God" and was taken up by the Space People to another planet where he was needed. I am firmly convinced that you and I can and will realize the same privilege in due time.

Human beings of the "mass-minded" category, naturally wake up in the next Density when they die. They then only possess the finer Etheric or Astral body, having moved out of the denser physical body --and "lost it" because of having broken the "Silver Cord". They are then known as "spirits". But here is the important thing to realize: The mere fact that a person becomes a "spirit" does not necessarily make him or her a "superbeing" all at once. Not at all. A "spirit" or "departed one" still remains much the same as he did before his transition. That is, he has the same mental attitude that he had on Earth. However, due to the fact that the molecules that make up the Etheric worlds obey laws different from those governing matter on Earth, a "spirit" has to study those laws and then learn how to apply them properly.

It is only through mastering all the natural laws that govern Atmospherea, that a spirit being, or "departed one" is able to progress to the next higher density. That is to Etherea, or the Third Density of etheric matter.

The Ethereans dwell in etheric regions which extend above and beyond Atmospherea. They possess much finer etheric bodies than do the Atmosphereans. Etherean angels are beautiful, glorified beings. They are often called "Celestials". Mentally, they express an extremely high order of intelligence. In fact, so intelligent are they that they are allowed to govern certain stars, planets and worlds. But here is the interesting point:

As stated previously, all etheric beings still function in bodies made of physical matter. True, it is much finer than material we see on earth. Nevertheless, angels must retain bodies of extremely fine matter until the time comes for them to make their next "upward" spiritual step.

In the meantime, while they are learning important lessons of life in Etherea, the people of that world make use of "Fire-Ships" or Space Discs, to fly on important missions. These vehicles (also called "Ether Ships") are built by the Spacecraft Constructors of Etherea and Atmospherea, to carry the inhabitants from place to place. In this manner the angels of the lower and higher heavens learn the secrets of the Universe.

There is much magic connected with the Ether Ships and their operation. That is, it appears to be "magic" to us Earthlings, for we do not as yet comprehend it fully. It is only magical to us until we can gain greater knowledge of the HOW and the WHY of it.

In the book OAHSPE you will find many enlightening descriptions of Ether Ships. As most students of Saucer Phenomena are aware, the motive power for some of these discs is produced by musical sound activated by the action of the pilot's will-power.

For instance, on page 209 in the section relating to Fragapatti, Son of Jehovih, Chapter XIII, Paragraph 4, we read:

"Now struck up the Ethereans with music, thirty thousand of them, but soft and gentle as a breath of wind, carrying the tones around about the SHIP, even as an endless echo, calling and answering from all possible directions, a continuous and enrapturing change, as if near, and as if far off. So that the uninformed knew not whence the music came nor how it was produced.

"All these things were set to working order just as the great Avalanza (Ether Ship) was ready to start. Then Fragapatti went into the ship, being almost the last one to enter. Already the light was gathering bright and dense about him, his head almost hid in the brilliancy of the halo. And then he called out:

"Arise! Arise! In Jehovih's name, upward rise! And as he spake, behold the avalanza MOVED WITH HIS WILL, for all the hosts (student angels) joined in the same expression, and presently started upward the great Fire-Ship; leaving the burning walls and signal centres flickering below, so that even hell overthrown shone with great grandeur."

Again, on page 317, from the section relating to Openta-Armij, Daughter of Jehovih, Paragraph 19, we find:

"By music alone, some their ships propelled, the vibratory chords affording power sufficient in such high-skilled hands, and the tunes changing according to the regions traversed. Others, even by colors made in the waves of sound, went forward, carrying millions of angels, every one attuned so perfectly that his very presence lent power and beauty to that monarch vessel."

We should realize that, just as there are a great variety of different makes and models of automobiles and airplanes here on Earth, likewise, there exist a million varieties of Spacecraft (including Ether Ships). Some are in the shape of silvery discs. Some are cigar shaped. Some resemble bells, with a super-structure (see George Adamski's book, "Flying Saucers Have Landed"). Still others may have strange forms as yet unknown to us.. However, Ether Ships have power to become visible and invisible. They can appear and disappear. Spacecraft from other denser physical planets remain visible to the eye. That is, they are visible when moving at slow speeds, or when hovering, or when they have landed.

Of course, it is obvious that any interplanetary craft, regardless of whether it is of physical or etheric construction, becomes increasingly less visible the faster it travels. After a Flying Saucer, for example, has reached maximum acceleration it is moving at the speed of 186,000 miles per second. This is the rate of speed attained by light, so the effect produced by a material object that attains that velocity would be something like a streak of light.

In future Mystic Monographs, we shall have more to say about the higher "life levels"--Atmospherea and Etherea--which will open up many new doors of understanding to you. You will be taught how to make certain of your "graduation" from Atmospherea (the next Density) in the briefest time possible, so that you can move up and away from the 2nd Density and into the 3rd Density of Etherea.

I am sure you will agree that it is foolish for any intelligent being to settle for anything less than the best in life. As an instance of this, why be satisfied with HALF-WAY answers to the many important questions you have about life and about yourself? Why not dig a little beneath the "surface" of things and find out some of the REAL REASONS for the seemingly "mysterious" happenings that go on?

All things can be explained...in a way that satisfies both the mind and the soul. Every effect has a CAUSE. You are learning some of the really important causes right now. You are getting acquainted with a much larger universe now; and you can see that you will have many exciting and thrilling NEW lessons to master when you yourself are one day ready to take your place in the higher Heaven Worlds.

"THE MAGIC OF ETHER SHIPS"

Part Two

The Great Harvest

Our planet Earth is on a mystical journey through space. That is what our scientists mean when they say that we live in an "expanding universe". Our Solar System with all its planets, moons and stars, is moving constantly upward and outward into higher regions of cosmic space.

One of these regions is known by the name of "Dan" which means "Light". In this region are found some of the higher Etherean kingdoms. Therefore, our Earth must move through the regions of Dan, as it spirals onward and ever outward in space and time.

We are entering the Regions of Dan now. Consequently, you and I are living in the "Time of Dan", and so are receiving higher spiritual vibrations from this Region as our Earth rotates through it.

Quite naturally, the influence of this higher Etheric Realm upon mortals on Earth is considerable. That is why more and more men and women in all walks of life, and of all ages, are "looking to the sky" and to the Space People, for spiritual wisdom. Many people are puzzled over the things that are "coming upon the earth". They do not have even a slight "inkling" of what is in store for our world and its inhabitants.

As you well know, the subject of "Flying Saucers" is no longer something to be ridiculed or "laughed away". So many people have seen the Discs that mankind is finally waking up to the fact that "there are more things in heaven and earth....than are dreamed of in our philosophies" as Shakespeare said. We are beginning to accept Flying Discs and Spacemen as a reality to be considered. That is good. Of course, students of the mystic and occult side of nature have known about Flying Discs and similar phenomena for hundreds and thousands of years. We have long recognized "Saucers" for what they are: portents of THE COMING SPIRITUAL AGE!

A most illuminating occult explanation of Ether Ships and their mystic purpose, is revealed to us in the Book of Jehovih, from OAHSPE. Paragraph 13 tells us:

"And God shall appoint Chiefs under him who shall go down and dwell on the Earth with mortals; and such Chiefs" labor shall be with mortals for their RESURRECTION. And these Chiefs shall be called Lords, for they are Gods of Land, which is the lowest rank of My commissioned Gods.

"And God and his Lords shall have dominion from 200 years to 1000 or more years; but never more than 3000 years. (Length of Minor Cycle). According to the regions of Dan (Light) into which I

<u>bring the Earth</u>, so shall be the terms of the office of My Gods and My Lords.

"And God and His Lords shall raise up officers to be their successors; by Him and by them shall they be appointed and crowned in My Name.

"At the termination of the dominion of My God and His Lords shall gather together in these My bound heavens, all such angels as have been prepared in wisdom and strength for resurrection to My Etherean Kingdoms. And these angels shall be called Brides and Bridegrooms to Jehovih, for they are Mine and in My service.

"And to God and his Lords, with the Brides and Bridegrooms, will I send <u>down from Etherea SHIPS</u> (Ether Ships) <u>in the time of Dan</u>; by My Etherean Gods and Goddesses shall the ships descend to these heavens, and receive God and His Lords with the Brides and Bridegrooms, and carry them up to the exalted regions I have prepared for them.

"And all such as ascend shall be called a Harvest unto Me through My God and Lords."

The "Chiefs" who come down to the Earth and dwell with mortals, are the Space People who are still "in the Flesh". That is, they are not returning from the dead for they never died. By occult knowledge they continued living on in the same bodies as of this earth. In other words, the "Chiefs" have conquered that last enemy called "Death".

Their purpose is to teach all mortals who have proven themselves worthy of such knowledge, that they too can conquer Death. However, immortality of the physical body will only be realized by progressive individuals who are capable of attaining it. We must remember that "many are called, but few are chosen". This applies here also.

As you have already noted, millions of human beings now living on Earth will NOT survive the next 45 years physically. They will--due to one cause of another--pass out of physical embodiment before the next era of Peace and Plenty (The Millenium) arrives. Among these millions of souls will be many wonderful people, men and women who are highly evolved individuals. The mere fact that they had to pass through the experience called Death does not mean that they are inferior beings. Actually, many of them will be the "cream of the crop" of mortals. They simply neglected to study the important science of "Immortality" during Earth Life.

What then, will happen to these people? According to the book of Jehovih, they will, after death, find themselves dwelling in the heavens of Atmospherea, the next Density beyond the material Earth. There they will remain until the "Time of Dan", which occurs frequently (once every several hundred years). Then, the "Great Harvest" of Angels takes place in the heaven worlds.

The Ethereans descend in their Ether Ships to "Harvest" the "Elect" or good souls in Atmospherea. Then the Ethereans ascend with several million new angels which have been "emancipated" from Atmospherea (the lower heavens) and enter into the higher heavens of Etherea...the Celestial Realm.

As we mentioned previously, our planet is moving into the higher etheric regions at this very moment, and has been doing so for the past ten years. Consequently, the "Great Harvest" is on right now in the Etheric kingdoms. The Ethereans are intensely active in the "Second Density" (Atmospherea) collecting into their Fire-Ships all those who are prepared for the great new journey which is onward, upward and Godward into the Third Density or Etherea.

Why use Ether Ships for this purpose? Why do spirits or angels require anything as cumbersome as a "Space Ship" in order to go from one place to another in the etheric realms? Why not just fly with their spirit body and soar up into the higher kingdoms?

The answer is, the astral bodies of the people living in Atmospherea, the lower heaven world, are much too densified to be able to function comfortably in Etherea. You might liken this situation to deep sea diving. If we send a diver down into the extreme depths of the ocean, we have to protect his body by encasing it in a special diving suit built to withstand the pressure below. Now, once our diver reaches the levels of the ocean, we must NOT bring him up to the surface of the water suddenly or he will suffer extreme pain. He may even develop a condition known as the "bends", if he is moved too rapidly from high pressure to low pressure. Again, fishes of the deep-sea variety are known to burst when brought up into the upper levels of the ocean water.

The environmental differences between Density 1 (material earth) Density 2 (Atmospherea) and Density 3 (Etherea) are so pronounced, some means of protection must be afforded to bodies of those who attempt to oove freely through those densities.

Ether Ships are the logical solution to this problem of transportation between the 2nd Density and Etherea. In the first place, Ether Ships are not cumbersome or unwieldy as would be, for example, our jet planes or six motored transport planes or even our helpful helicopters. Instead, Ether Ships are sleek, smooth, luxurious vessels which glide through space serenely and peacefully.

In the second place, although those persons who experienced "death" on earth, and who are now living in Atmospherea, are able to "fly" with ease through the Atmosphere of that Density (including our own material density of earth), they cannot fly beyond the uppermost spacial regions of Atmospherea. To do so would cause them much pain. I am speaking now of flights in the etheric or "astral" body only, without the use of Spacecraft of any kind. So you see that even those individuals living in the next Density (atmospherea) are limited the same as you and I, though not to the same extent. The point s, they _do_ have their limitations, and must observe them.

Human beings, that is, Earthlings, who have developed their spiritual sight through certain occult practices, are able to clairvoyantly SEE the Ether Ships as they descend into Atmospherea for the "Great Harvest". As you now realize, this is happening more and more frequently as we move into the higher etheric regions of light.

Many persons assert they have seen Ether Ships which seemed to appear and disappear at will. I have been asked many times for my opinion as to how such phenomena occurs. My reply has always been, that since the Ethereans are more highly evolved beings mentally and spiritually than we are at this time, it is no great trick for them to "materialize" and "dematerialize" their spacecraft. All that is required for an etherean ship to suddenly become visible to us, is a change in the "molecular polarity" of the ship. This could be done by _mind force_ or by electronic means. The ship would then "attract" denser physical matter to it, causing it to "appear".

On the other hand, by reversing this particular polarity, the ship again returns to its original condition of "invisibility" because it is made of _finer-etheric matter_ than we are accustomed to seeing physically.

Summing up what we have been talking about in the last two or three pages, there are several general conclusions we can arrive at in regard to the "Ether Ships".

1. They are designed to transport the good souls from Atmospherea into Etherea. This being accomplished once every several hundred years. It is the "Great Harvest".

2. They are specially "pressurized" spacecraft of finer etheric density than other spacecraft from material densities. As the chosen atmospherean angels (the host) are transported upward into higher regions of etherean space, they are assisted by the Ethereans to "raise their vibrations" so they will be able to dwell comfortably in Etherea.

3. Without Ether Ships millions of souls dwelling in Atmospherea would never be able to leave the 2nd Density and progress higher into the 3rd Density of Etherea.

4. They (Ether Ships) have the power to become visible or invisible to our eyes. A good illustration of this power is given in OAHSPE, book of Sethantes, page 24, paragraphs 8 & 9. I quote:

"When the ship of the hosts of God came to the city of Uldoo, mortals _SAW it high up in the air_, and they feared and ran hastily to consult the prophet of the Lord. And the prophet said: Behold, God appeareth in a sea of fire (glowing ether ship) in the firmament of Heaven.

"And God caused the Ship to be made unseen, that fear might subside on earth, and he descended with his hosts into the house of the Lord, and they went and touched the things mortals had builded that they might perceive corporeally."

5. Ether Ships are NOT the same craft that come from Venus, Mars, and other dense worlds much like our own planet. Instead, they come from another dimension entirely...namely, the 4-dimensional Space-Time world of Etherea, which is one of the etheric or invisible worlds interpenetrating Earth.

Due to the fact that the Ethereans are beings of a higher dimensional world, they may not look very much like us Earth Folk when they are functioning in their natural "habitat". However, when they come into a denser plane to carry out some good mission, they use bodies just like we do. Of course, they might be a little taller or shorter possibly--but much more attractive and with a much greater spiritual understanding than we have.

At the present time the general public is largely "in the dark" regarding the Ether Ship mystery. Most people have heard, read about or actually seen "Flying Saucers"--which are NOT Ether Ships, as we have learned in this study. However, few persons have discovered the story of these INTERDIMENSIONAL CRAFT that originate in Etheric Realms!

Quite true, the newspapers, the radio, and television reporters are "playing down" the whole astounding episode. There is an enforced "hush-hush" rule among the newscasters. The idea is to treat "Flying Saucers" and Spacemen" as one big joke, and then let it go at that. On the other hand, only a very few of them are even aware of such things as "Ether Ships" or the etheric realms.

So the Discs will have to do their own talking. This they are doing more and more. Some of the true story will be told to the "mass-minded" in the late Spring of 1956. Our Space Friends--for such in truth they are--will then gently help our fellow humans on Earth to "grow up" in short order, by presenting thousands of Earthlings with objective "phenomena" that simply can't be explained away. Time, as you know, is short. We are living in the prophesied "time of the End". It is time for a CHANGE.

Fortunately, our planetary Guardians are waking us up. They are filling our skies with an ever increasing number of space ships from many different Densities. "Contacts" by Earthlings like George Adamski, Truman Bethurum, Orfeo Angelucci, Dan Frey, and others, with the Space People are becoming commonplace. We are learning to face " "reality" and the tempo of this learning is being stepped-up dramatically by our great teachers.

In the coming years, people on Earth will tremble with fear of "the things that are coming upon the Earth". . . . You, however, will not tremble. In those moments of terrible darkness and indecision, you will not panic. We who believe in God understand that he created ALL the heavens and the Earth. By "heavens" we understand that to mean the entire universe all the way out to the last star. This includes planets beyond planets, suns beyond suns, solar systems beyond solar systems, galaxies beyond galaxies.

Too, we know that means the UNSEEN WORLDS as well as the seen. Let us accept the Creator in His fullness...in all His Infinite Glory. When we do this, and we shall--what would we have to fear? In truth, there is nothing at all to fear. The entire universe is FOR man, not against him. All things work together for GOOD, and even though the Earth itself be "removed out of her place" so that she "reels to and fro like a drunkard"...still our hearts shall NOT fail us. Intelligence, not chaos, rules the universe.

And it is the intelligence in you that can and will protect you now and in the perilous days to come, just as it has always stood by to direct you during serious times in the past. You have done nobly well, and my only suggestion would be to practice living more and more from your own Soul-Center of Life, Love and Light in your daily activities. Therein lies your only true security.

Of course, many of the Space People are your friends. This includes many of the Ethereans as well. They are spiritually evolved enough to know that all evil is self-destructive and consequently of no use whatsoever to the illumined soul. However, evil is by no means confined to planet Earth exclusively. Wherever life exists, there also exists the possibility of misusing that life. Hence we can expect to find evil-doers on any planet, no matter how highly advanced or evolved the people of that planet might be. While it is true the majority of the Visitors from Space are constructively minded, there are a few who are not. And it is for this reason that we must "test" every being whom we contact (or who contacts us) to find out if he is on the side of Cosmic Good or mere personal gain.

I believe that in this Monograph I have givin you a new and more comprehensive picture of THE REAL YOU and your ever-unfolding spiritual destiny. We have delved deeply into the ancient lore of that mystic Land known as ETHERIA. We've seen how the Ethereans are able to function efficiently in their Etheric Realms, by living there according to the physical, mental and spiritual laws of their higher dimensional worlds. We have uncovered much of the mystery surrounding ETHER SHIPS, learned why they are necessary, and we have caught a glimpse of our own great and wondrous journey to the stars.

We've come to know that your journey and mine, is ever Onward, Upward and Godward...from Density to Density...higher and higher... until at last one day our minds comprehend Creation in its grandly magnificent aspects. Then we will have returned on the "ingoing wave" to the One Still Light at the center of All.

Discs, Destiny & You

by

MICHAEL X

Mystic Monograph No. 5

A PERSONAL NOTE

Dear Friend and Mystic Student:

In this Monograph, "DISCS, DESTINY & YOU", we study a subject of vital interest and importance to all of us. That is, the COMING COLLOSAL CHANGES which our planet Terra (and its 3 billion people) are due to experience between now and the Golden Millenium we are joyously awaiting.

Your Destiny during the next 44 years will be far more thrilling, enlightening, and "adventurous" than you--at this moment--can possibly imagine. Yes. It will be a wonderful Destiny, because of the profound influence for good the Space People are going to have on your life from now on.....in spite of the "changes" that must transpire.

The secret of staying "alive" (that is, in physical embodiment) from now on, even through the eventual crisis to come, is to change your thought and keep it changed. For those who start at once improving their mental world by thinking along the lines of Love, Life, Truth and Beauty, the future will be exceedingly bright. Few of the unpleasant things, such as the cataclysmic changes impending, or the axial SHIFT of the earth as revealed in these pages, will even affect those whose feet are on the glorious Mystic Path leading Upward.

Positive Thought-Control, however, is imperative. The old mental patterns of fear, negation, and destructive emotion, cannot be taken into the coming Millenium, which will be the INTERPLANETARY AGE. As space flight becomes a reality to Earthlings, a New Order of thinking will awaken on Earth, in which we will have related ourselves more perfectly to the magnificent purposes of the Creator of all Life.

Yours in Truth and Love,

Michael X

MICHAEL X

MYSTIC MONOGRAPH   NUMBER FIVE

"DISCS, DESTINY AND YOU"

Part One

The Polar Shift

Flying Discs, the Space People, and our Earth's polar "shift", are all related in a most interesting way, to your Destiny. Destiny is that which is irrevocable. That is, it is an experience or combination of experiences which you must become "aware" of as you move forward in consciousness.

Death, for example, is a form of destiny which all mankind (with the exception of a very few Adepts) learns to accept mentally. In fact, race thought has it that death is inevitable for all living creatures. Those who study the mystic science of mind, life, and spirit, learn that destiny is not always "unchangeable". We can be "Masters of Fate".

Occult science defines destiny as "necessity"; that which must be or happen as the result of what has been thought and said or done in the past or present time. Your destiny, then, has little or nothing to do with "stars" or where you happen to live, or even whom you happen to meet "by chance". Instead, we create our own individual destinies day by day, moment by moment--BY THE KIND OF THOUGHTS WE THINK.

Change your mind--your "consciousness"--and you change your destiny. The idea is to change your thoughts from negative to positive, from destructive to constructive, and by so doing you are creating a NEW "chain of events" that will brighten your tomorrows. We can never hope to enjoy happy experiences in the future unless we lay the foundations today, by our present thoughts and actions.

Many students of the Inner Teachings believe in an "ultimate destiny". That is, they feel that some day, some time, they will experience a FINAL or LAST destiny. For some persons the ultimate destiny would be to attain "Cosmic Consciousness" or to be absorbed in an ecstatic, blissful state of "Nirvana". According to the Space People, man has NO ultimate or final destiny. There is no such thing as FINALITY in all the Cosmos. We do, however, have an INFINITE DESTINY. You and I are now thinking beings. As a result of our thoughts, we are continually creating a moving "Succession" of destinies for ourselves. Since you never cease "unfolding", how could there be a final destiny?

Once you realize this, you instantly become more of a master over yourself and over life itself. The principle of it all is utterly simple and sensible. One doesn't have to go anywhere else or seek somebody outside of himself, to bring about this INNER Change of Consciousness. One has merely to ask himself (or herself) "Which do I serve? Good or Evil? The Unlimited or the Limited?" In your choice lies your Destiny-to-be.

Good is unlimited in its scope of action, whereas Evil tends to destroy itself. One is an expanding force; the other contracting. If you contract anything, it soon dies. Life simply refuses to be confined, restricted or contracted in any way. The tendency of the entire Universe is E-X-P-A-N-S-I-O-N. We live in an "expanding universe". In this principle is found the real key to abundant living.

I mention these things because they do have an important bearing on your own Destiny, which will soon be apparent to you. At this particular moment, time is "of the essence". In order to properly construct the best kind of destiny for yourself in this changing world, it is necessary to know the facts.

Occultists have long known of the existence of "planetary cycles". Ancient Hindu writings such as the Book of Dzyan, describe these cycles in detail. It seems that each planet, including our Earth, experiences a number of "axial shifts" during its lifetime. These shifts occur with a certain regularity, which the ancients claim to have measured with some degree of exactness. For example, "Racial Cycles" which measure the progress of man on Earth, are figured in a Minor Cycle (2500--3000 years) and a Major Cycle (26,000 years). Racial Cycles are related to Planetary Cycles.

A Planetary Cycle covers a period of 7200 years (round numbers). It is at the end of this period that the axis of the Earth makes a sudden SHIFT, causing the land to slide under the oceans at terrific speed, and tearing away mountains and covering forests. This happened not once, but many times ages ago, which fact accounts for our present coal beds. Also, it accounts for the presence of Mammoths (a tropical animal) being frozen in mountains of ice in the far north regions. The Mammoth belongs to the Elephant family, and elephants have an intense dislike for cold weather. Their natural habitat is in tropical regions, such as Africa and India. What history books call the "Glacial Period" or the "Ice Age", was a planetary condition which resulted from a polar shift.

This idea of a periodic "Polar Shift" was first brought to my attention by George Van Tassel during my last visit with him at Giant Rock. I think it would not be amiss to briefly review what was mentioned then. It was George's understanding that our Earth is now approaching the mid-point between a Minor and a Major Cycle. This seems to indicate that our planet is nearing the end of a Planetary Cycle (7200 years). The time remaining until the end of this Cycle is reached, is not exactly known; however, there is some evidence to the effect that this cycle will terminate within 45 years from today.

This does not mean that our world will "come to an end" at that time. Not at all. A periodic shift of the Earth's axis should occur at that time, just as it happened in the long-since-forgotten past.

Quite true, for a great number of people it will be the "end of the world", for they will not survive the tremendous planetary cataclysm.

The Space People, George said, are well aware of the Polar Shift that is in the offing. They realize fully that the general effect of atomic explosions on Earth is to hasten the "Time of the End", for the simple reason that--as Sir Isaac Newton observed--"For every action there is an opposite and equal reaction". Shoot a gun and the gun "kicks" back. Explode a Hydrogen Bomb on the Earth's surface and the Earth must also "react" by oscillating or "wobbling" more in its orbit. This has already occurred.

The "wobble" takes place at the extreme ends of the earth where the polar ice caps are located. This ice forms a mountain two miles high. In fact, both the North and the South Poles are surrounded by many millions of square miles of polar ice. As the earth spins around describing its large orbit, the polar ice caps also rotate..but in small eccentric ellipse. This small "eccentric orbit" is spread out over the larger one. Therefore the Earth actually describes TWO orbits AT THE SAME TIME, in place of merely one. Now, if we increase the diameter of the smaller orbit, what happens?

The "gyroscopic" action of the earth increases, does it not? As a result, the polar ice caps MELT AT A MUCH FASTER RATE. When those "mountains of ice" two miles high, begin to melt rapidly they SHIFT THEIR WEIGHT. This condition causes definite land and climatical changes to occur all over the Earth.

The severe polar shift occurs when the "wobble" of the poles reaches an extreme or maximum state of imbalance. Then, like a gyroscope trying to right itself, a sudden BIG SHIFT takes place and land crumples and slides under the oceans with violent speed.

George Van Tassel believes that this is the time referred to in the Christian Bible as "The Father's house-cleaning among the planets" During this critical time of the "Great Shift", or immediately before this world event, our friends from space will descend in their Flying Discs and other Space Ships, to rescue all deserving humanity.

There is a story told of Abe Lincoln that seems to be appropriate at this point. As you know, the woods are full of "false prophets" who go about predicting the "end of the world". Usually, when the prophesied time arrives, nothing happens...and the Earth keeps on rolling around just as if it hadn't any idea that--according to prophecy--it was supposed to "be consumed" in one way or another.

One day a group of Lincoln's friends ran up to him in great excitement, exclaiming, "The world is coming to an end! The world is coming to an end!"

Honest Abe didn't appear the least bit disturbed by the news. His friends tried again to impress the situation on his mind.

"Don't you understand?" they shouted, "The whole world is coming to an end NOW!"

Lincoln looked them in the eye. "That's all right, boys," he said. "I can get along without the world!"

We can learn much from Lincoln's calm reaction to "startling" news. It tells us that he had found his own spiritual center of serenity which nothing outside of himself could shake...for his REAL SELF was IMMORTAL.

****

A VISION OF THE IMPENDING

"Destruction is but the prelude to Renewal:
Death is but the portal to Life;
Even truth also must be made new,
Behold, I saw the Heaven in a blaze of purity,
And I saw the EARTH absorbed into an Abyss.
THE ROLLING SPHERE INCLINED!

"The moment of destruction was at hand.
Mountains suspended over mountains;
Hills sinking upon hills;
Lofty trees toppled headlong;
They sank downwards into chasms."

--The Book of Enoch

SPECIAL NOTE

Due to the unusual and Occult nature of the various subjects presented in MYSTIC Monographs, they should be considered as confidential. The purchaser is requested to maintain the ancient Occult Law of Silence as regards all Secret Knowledge, lest it fall into unworthy hands. If you do wish to lend them to close friends, first ascertain the sincerity of the one desiring this knowledge.   The Author.

"DISCS, DESTINY & YOU"

Part Two

Your Secret Destiny

As soon as I became aware that a "shift" in the axis of the earth was impending, I at once began a diligent search for more facts. What I found was, to say the least, as astounding as it was enlightening. All of the ancient esoteric teachings were in agreement on one momentous and important thing:

THE AXIS OF THIS EARTH PERIODICALLY INCLINES AT A 45 DEGREE ANGLE TO THE PLANE OF ITS ORBIT, AND IT HAS GONE THROUGH FOUR SUCH INCLINATIONS DURING PAST AGES.

Or, to put it more simply, the axis of rotation shifts suddenly, causing the earth to tip at an angle of 45 degrees. Ever since the first dawn of creation, man has observed that our globe has a unique "cyclical" life of its own. That is why the belief is expressed in nearly all the old writings (history, mythology, philosophy and Occult manuscripts) that this Earth has passed through a series of time cycles, each cycle ending in a "planetary convulsion" such as a violent earthquake, a flood, volcanic fire explosion, etc. The Deluge is but one instance.

The Rosicrucians firmly believe that the earth inclines or "tips" at regular intervals. They have given us much valuable literature on this vital subject, and I heartily recommend that you look into the late Max Heindel's book, "The Rosicrucian Cosmo-Conception" for much worthwhile information on this. A copy of the book can usually be obtained at your public library, or from an Occult book store.

As we have noted previously in another Monograph of this series, fire and water alternately destroy the continents of Earth. The active agents in this destruction being earthquakes, volcanoes, tornadoes, sinkings and displacements of the various land areas. These periodical cataclysms of our planet do not, however, happen without warning. In every case of the earth "shifting" on its axis and tipping sharply, humanity is kindly given a number of "warnings" beforehand. I refer, of course, to incessant earthquakes and volcanic eruptions which occur years in advance of the major devastating "shift."

Commentaries in the Secret Doctrine mention one of these events as follows:

"The great mother (Earth) travailed under the waves and a new land was joined to the first one which our wise men called the headgear (North Pole). She travailed harder for the third (race) and her waist and navel appeared above the water. It was the belt, the sacred Himavat, which stretches around the world. She broke toward the setting sun from her neck downward (to the southwest) into many lands and islands, but the eternal land (the cap) broke not asunder. Dry lands covered the face of the silent waters to the four sides of the world. All these perished. Then appeared the abode of the wicked (Atlantis). The eternal land was now hid, for the waters became solid (frozen) under the breath of her nostrils and evil winds from the Dragon's mouth," etc., etc.

This account as well as all of the other old and dusty manuscripts which describe the periodical tip of the earth, reveal the ancient belief that the North Pole was our first and original continent on Earth. At the beginning of creation, the "eternal land" was NOT a place of ice and snow as it is today. Instead, it was a veritable tropical paradise, much like the State of Florida is now.

The original "Garden of Eden"--where man was first created on this planet--was located in that continent at the North Pole. Later came the great "polar shift", reversing the climatic conditions completely, and freezing the tropical Mammoth Elephant in mountains of ice two miles high.

Delving still deeper into the ancient books, we find another astounding manuscript on this intensely fascinating subject. It is the Commentary of an old Buddhist Faith as cited by Blavatsky:

"When the wheel (Earth) runs at the usual rate, its extremities (the poles) agree with its middle circle (equator). When it runs slower and tilts in every direction, there is a great disturbance on the face of the earth. The waters flow toward the two ends, and new lands arise in the middle belt, while those at the ends are subject to pralayas (cleansing) by submersion."

You have quite likely heard of the "Book of Enoch". It is a Biblical book, yet it pre-dates our Bible by millions of years. Some Bible commentators refer to it as the "Book of Adam", for they are of the opinion that Adam wrote it. One chapter is titled "A Sermon to the Sons of Men". It seems to be describing a vision of THE COMING CRISIS of our planet, now impending. I quote:

"Yet all this starry firmament of beauty shall pass away, and cease to be in the days to come; they shall be changed by FIRE; they shall be renovated by WATER, as of old in the olden time. GOD shall come forth out of the places afar off; He will tread upon the mountains, and the mountains shall give way under Him, and the valleys shall be made straight before His feet, and the pillars of the earth shall be shaken; the Voice of the Supreme shall be heard; the mighty Heaven shall hear and tremble; the sea and waves shall quake with terror.

"The sun shall not be visible; the moon shall also withold her light; but there shall be NO DEATH, NOR ANY DESTRUCTION: but all shall be renovated and made more beautiful than ever."--Book of Enoch.

It is difficult to see how there would be no death for the masses of humankind when the earth next tips at a 45 degree angle. I think we may safely interpret that passage to mean there shall be no death

FOR THE ELECT of "Enlightened" and spiritual people...who are now launched on the UPWARD PATH.

That, in fact, is your SECRET DESTINY. You and I and an ever-increasing number of sincere individuals--men, women and children in all walks of life--can be comforted in the knowledge that, when the time of the "Great Tribulation" comes (and no man knoweth the day nor the hour) many wise and highly spiritual beings will descend to this planet in Flying Discs. Their purpose: to preserve as many human beings in the physical state as possible. All else will find no protection.

The Space People from Venus (the planet which represents our Earth's "higher self") are God's messengers of Light. We should trust them, as we would trust God. That is to say, we should embrace the help they offer whenever they choose to offer it. And we need NOT fear them, nor need we live in dread of the next polar shift, for:

"God is our refuge and strength, a very present <u>help</u> in trouble. Therefore will we NOT FEAR, though the Earth be removed, and though the mountains be carried into the midst of the sea; though the waters thereof roar and be troubled, though the mountains shake with the SWELLING thereof."................Psalm 46: 1-3

That advice is from our own Bible, and I am sure you recognize it. Also, I do trust that its real meaning is conveyed to you more clearly than when you previously read it. The connection between the Space People, that is, the Venusians, and the "Polar Shift" is seen in another Biblical passage:

"And when these things begin to come to pass, then LOOK UP, and LIFT UP YOUR HEADS; for your redemption (protection) draweth nigh."
Luke 21: 28

What does this mean? It means that our "way of escape" from destruction in the Dark Night of Tribulation, is simply not to stay on the earth during the cataclysm, but to allow our friends (the Space People) to lift us up off the planet in their Space Ships.

When the earth has once again righted itself, and the sun and moon again show their light...we shall be returned safely to this planet, to experience the glorious Millenium. In the words of our own Bible, "Then we which are alive and remain (in the flesh) shall be caught up together with them in the clouds, to meet the Lord in the air; and so shall we ever be with the Lord." (That is, under the guiding influence of the Venusians)........Thess. 4: 16, 17

Those of us who are fully aware of the possibility of this event coming to pass in the not too distant future, will not hesitate to prepare ourselves mentally, physically and spiritually for it... NOW.

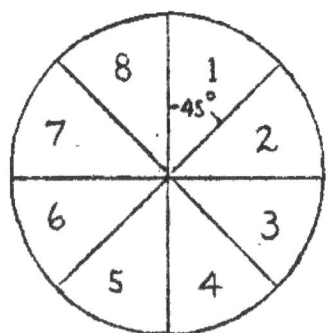

Bozena Brydlova, author of a most enlightening book entitled, "The Brydlovan Theory of the Origin of Numbers", gives us much valuable information on the Great Shift:

"All the data contained within the old philosophies teach us that man attained his development in Cycles, beginning with senseless innocence and purity, and gradually developing from acquired materialism AFTER EACH TIP OF THE EARTH, into a state of degradation. When the lowest state of degradation has been reached, the wheel starts its way UPWARD and once more humanity treads the UPWARD PATH, higher with each tip of the axis, until the time that ALL are gathered to the One Cause thru their spiritual attainment of purity. Precise figures as to the length of time from tip to tip give us 7200 years. Dividing the cosmic circle into 45 degree angles, we find four on one side and four on the other. True it is that mankind could hardly reach a lower state of humanity than the world has witnessed in the past thousand years, but as we are said to be now in the FIFTH "sun" (fifth age), we can be comforted by the knowledge that we are NOW launched on the UPWARD PATH."

If this theory is correct, our earth has four more "tips" to make before it finally "etherializes", that is, turns into a sun.

What we call the "Millenium" was called the "Sibylline year" by Virgil. In his 4th Eclogue, he refers to the next tip of the earth.. and to the Millenium to follow:

"The last period sung by the Sibylline prophetess is now arrived and the grand series of Ages, that series which recurs again and again in the course of one mundane revolution, begins afresh. Now the Virgin Astraea returns from Heaven, and the primaeval reign of Venus recommences. Now a new race descends (in space ships) from the celestial realms of holiness. Do thou, Lucina, smile propituous on the birth of a Boy who will bring to a close the present age of Iron, and introduce throughout the whole world a new Age of Gold. Then shall the herds no longer dread the fury of the lion, nor shall the poison of the serpent any longer be formidable.

"Every venomous animal and every deleterious plant shall perish together. (As a result of the next axial shift). The fields shall be yellow with corn; the grapes shall hand in ruddy clusters from the bramble, and honey shall distill spontaneously from the rugged oak. The universal globe shall enjoy the blessings of PEACE, secure under the mild sway of its new and divine sovereign."

Delving back still further into the manuscripts of the ancients, we come to the Koran of the Mohammedans. Here again we find a descriptive account of the next "shift": "The earth shall be SHAKEN, and not only all the buildings, but THE VERY MOUNTAINS LEVELED, and THE HEAVENS MELTED, etc."

To banish whatever trace of skepticism yet remains in your mind, as to the actual TRUTH of the several "axial shifts" already made by our planet, consider the following:

On the great Sahara desert, sea-shells in numerous quantities can be found today...showing that this vast desert was formerly the bottom of an ancient ocean.

Yet another instance of this is found in Wyoming. Certain portions of that state are filled with petrified sea-shells; again proving that this now arid land was once an ocean bed. So we see that the "Great Shift" of the earth upon its axis, really did happen in the dim, bygone past...and not just once, but many times. At least four to date.

But what about NOW...today? Exactly what is happening to this planet right now? Fate Magazine for April 1955, on page 8, gave us some amazing data, which I quote:

"A slip amounting to about 75 feet a year has been detected between the earth's outer skin and her inner core. Whatthis may mean isn't known exactly, but it could help explain the suggested SHIFTING OF THE CONTINENTS under the continental drift theory.

"And besides all this, THE EARTH IS SHOWING AN INCREASING TIP IN HER AXIS. At present the pole seems to be shifting only about a centimeter a year...nearly 100 years to shift a yard...but the TILT SEEMS TO BE INCREASING and some estimates place the change as much as 10 centimeters a year.

"All this has been reported by Dr. Roger R. Revelle of the U.S. National Research Council and Dr. Walter H. Munk of the Scripps Institute of Oceanography, both of La Jolla, California."

This condition of the planet is causing drastic weather changes all over the globe. In 1953, William J. Baxter made a study of these climatic changes, and published his findings in a book titled, "Today's Revolution in The Weather". So popular was the book it sold 225,000 copies. In that book, Mr. Baxter brought the world weather situation to the attention of human beings everywhere. Now he has written an entirely new book on the same theme, entitled, "Warmer Weather!...Boom in North!" His thought is as follows:

"IT ISN'T 'JUST YOUR IMAGINATION'! Winters are getting warmer; summers are hotter, drier, more unbearable. Every scientific study, every anxious report from worried farmers, bankers, ranchers, fruit growers, retailers, real estate and utility men confirms it. The CLIMATE OF THE WHOLE NORTHERN HEMISPHERE IS CHANGING DRASTICALLY. And here in the United States and Canada, we are on the verge of the greatest revolution in agriculture, industry and daily living that has ever been known."

We, as students of life's deeper secrets, can look back of these "outer effects" and see the occult (that is, hidden) reasons for all the changes. We realize that a NEW NORTH POLE is coming about. (This fact throws ocean navigators many miles off course when charting by means of the old maps, which are now virtually obsolete).

Yes, Earth is wobbling on her axis. A new "Polar Shift" is due. The precise date of the shift remains of course, a cosmic secret. But we know the great event is not too far in the distant future. What is happening in and on the earth at this very moment logically foretells the mighty upheavals of Nature that will take place when the sudden shift comes. A probable date is any time between now and the year 2000 A.D., when the Golden Age of the Millenium begins.

We know the coming shift is scientifically predictable, just as it is now scientifically possible to predict solar eclipses, weather conditions, high and low tides, the next date when a certain comet will appear in our skies, etc. etc., so is it possible to calculate with a high degree of accuracy when the next SHIFT of our planet will occur. In our opinion the greatest authority on this vital subject is Mr. Adam D. Barber of Washington D.C. Mr. Barber is an attorney at law, who has experimented with and studied the gyroscopic action of our solar system for over twenty years. This led him to the discovery of our earth's periodic shift, coming soon, which will bring upon humanity a catastrophe of major proportions. If you have not yet read his book, "THE COMING DISASTER", I strongly urge you to send for a copy of it now. The price is only $1.00. The information it contains will prove of superlative value to you in the days ahead. To get your copy of Mr. Barber's book, send one dollar to the following address: BARBER SCIENTIFIC FOUNDATION. P.O. BOX 3254, Washington 10, D.C.

If you are diligent in your application of New Age truths from now on, you will quite likely reach the Millenium "in the flesh", and get safely past the "shift" without the slightest bit of physical harm coming to you during the whole thrilling experience. But you must see to it that the "coverings of the Light" are removed from your mind and spirit. Then you shall know yourself as a true Godlike being and be ready to take your place in the Age of Peace, Power and Plenty.

In the days to come, you will be guided in THE WAY you are to go for your safety and further progress. Much hidden knowledge and valuable instruction will be given you...often in quite strange and, yes, mysterious ways; but always at THE time when you need guidance most. Hence, you need not concern yourself unduly with the future. The Space Masters have told us that our lives must function from the SOUL CENTER within us...NOW, in this eternal instant of Time...which has no beginning and no end. We are Eternal Beings, sublimely "centered" in the One All-Seeing Mind within. Outer events cannot shake us nor destroy what is forever unshakable and indestructible.

I say to you sincerely, you have unlimited majesty within you. Release it. For your future is as BIG as the Universe is boundless, and as grand as the dreams and hungering demand of your waking Soul.

THE SHAVER MYSTERY AND THE INNER EARTH

At long last the TRUTH about the most astounding mystery of our time can be told without unneeded psychic trimmings and destorted editing. Direct from the pen of Timothy Green Beckley comes the book that is officially approved by Richard Shaver himself.

In this volume you will learn the amazing truth as to the actual origin for the Flying Saucers and why they are coming to Earth.

You'll read some of the most hair-raising and chilling accounts ever put down on paper. Such as the disappearance of Steve Brodie and his capture by the Dero. Of attacks on surface people by various creatures whose existence cannot now be denied.

Chapters and comments by such researchers as:

Dr. T. Lobsang Rampa - Dand Howard - Rev. Frank Stranges

See actual maps showing the EXACT location of the mystical city of ice "Rainbow City" - Rare hand paintings of the Jersey Devil - Never before published photographs of Pre-Deluge Artifacts.

Introduction by the author of THEY KNEW TOO MUCH ABOUT FLYING SAUCERS - Gray Barker.

Appendix by Ray Palmer former editor of AMAZING STORIES who first published Shaver's astounding accounts.

THE SHAVER MYSTERY AND THE INNER EARTH is a large 8-1/2 x 11 volume of 125 pages, the largest of this format we have published. Copies now $5.00.

 **ALSO READ THESE STARTLING NEW BOOKS ON UFOS**

1. MY VISIT TO VENUS by Dr. T. Lobsang Rampa. Did the famed Tibetan Lama actually visit Venus, or did he travel there astrally? $2.00

2. FLYING SAUCERS ARE WATCHING YOU by John Sherwood. The book that puts you inside the great Michigan flap. Photos, illustrations, etc. $3.95

3. UFO WARNING by John Stuart. Beset by strange occult forces and terrible warnings the author encounters a lecherous monster. $3.95

4. WE MET THE SPACE PEOPLE by the Mitchell Sisters. Two young sisters discuss their contacts with aliens from Mars and Venus. $1.10

5. STRANGE CASE OF DR. M. K. JESSUP edited by Gray Barker. New evidence that Dr. Jessup was silenced by the "men in black". $3.95

6. THE RETURN OF GEORGE ADAMSKI by E. Buckle. 2 days after his death the controversial contactee is said to have made contact with an English gardner. Learn of poltergeist like beings kidnapping people from Earth. Strange phone calls and tape recordings containing alien voices, etc. $5.95

7. DOCUMENT 96 by Frank Martin Chase. Lavishly illustrated volume suggests some saucers may be built by terrestrials - maybe the Nazis! $5.00

8. FLYING SAUCERS IN THE BIBLE by Virginia Brasington. The Bible contains many accounts of visitations of space people. Beautifully and inspiringly written $3.95

9. THE BOOK OF SPACE SHIPS AND THEIR RELATIONSHIPS WITH THE EARTH, by the God of a Planet Near the Earth and Others. Space communications of particularly inspiring nature. $3.95

Order From
SAUCERIAN BOOKS
Box 2228
Clarksburg, W. Va. 26301
WRITE FOR COMPLETE BOOK LIST

Dear Sir:
Please send me Shaver Mystery & Inner Earth at $5.00.
Send me following books listed by number_____
Name_____
Address_____ City_____ State_____ Zip_____

www.ingramcontent.com/pod-product-compliance
Lightning Source LLC
Chambersburg PA
CBHW081236170426
43198CB00017B/2774